Teenage Sexuality

Opposing Viewpoints®

Tamara L. Roleff, *Book Editor*

David L. Bender, *Publisher*

Bruno Leone, *Executive Editor*

Bonnie Szumski, *Editorial Director*

Stuart Miller, *Managing Editor*

OPPOSING
VIEWPOINTS®
SERIES

Greenhaven Press, Inc., San Diego, California

Cover photo: EyeWire Studios

Library of Congress Cataloging-in-Publication Data

Teenage sexuality : opposing viewpoints / Tamara L. Roleff, book
   editor.
      p.   cm. — (Opposing viewpoints series)
   Includes bibliographical references and index.
   ISBN 0-7377-0524-8 (lib. : alk. paper) —
ISBN 0-7377-0523-X (pbk. : alk. paper)
   1. Teenagers—United States—Sexual behavior.
2. Teenagers—United States—Attitudes. 3. Teenage
pregnancy—United States. I. Roleff, Tamara L., 1959–   .
II. Opposing viewpoints series (Unnumbered)

HQ27.T38 2001
306.7'0835—dc21   00-020687
                                                              CIP

Every effort has been made to trace the owners of copyrighted material.

Greenhaven Press, Inc., P.O. Box 289009
San Diego, CA 92198-9009

Teenage Sexuality

Opposing Viewpoints®

Other Books of Related Interest

> "Congress shall make no law...abridging the freedom of speech, or of the press."

First Amendment to the U.S. Constitution

The basic foundation of our democracy is the First Amendment guarantee of freedom of expression. The Opposing Viewpoints Series is dedicated to the concept of this basic freedom and the idea that it is more important to practice it than to enshrine it.

Contents

Why Consider Opposing Viewpoints?

"The only way in which a human being can make some approach to knowing the whole of a subject is by hearing what can be said about it by persons of every variety of opinion and studying all modes in which it can be looked at by every character of mind. No wise man ever acquired his wisdom in any mode but this."

John Stuart Mill

In our media-intensive culture it is not difficult to find differing opinions. Thousands of newspapers and magazines and dozens of radio and television talk shows resound with differing points of view. The difficulty lies in deciding which opinion to agree with and which "experts" seem the most credible. The more inundated we become with differing opinions and claims, the more essential it is to hone critical reading and thinking skills to evaluate these ideas. Opposing Viewpoints books address this problem directly by presenting stimulating debates that can be used to enhance and teach these skills. The varied opinions contained in each book examine many different aspects of a single issue. While examining these conveniently edited opposing views, readers can develop critical thinking skills such as the ability to compare and contrast authors' credibility, facts, argumentation styles, use of persuasive techniques, and other stylistic tools. In short, the Opposing Viewpoints Series is an ideal way to attain the higher-level thinking and reading skills so essential in a culture of diverse and contradictory opinions.

In addition to providing a tool for critical thinking, Opposing Viewpoints books challenge readers to question their own strongly held opinions and assumptions. Most people form their opinions on the basis of upbringing, peer pressure, and personal, cultural, or professional bias. By reading carefully balanced opposing views, readers must directly confront new ideas as well as the opinions of those with whom they disagree. This is not to simplistically argue that everyone who reads opposing views will—or should—change his or her opinion. Instead, the series enhances readers' understanding of their own views by encouraging confrontation with opposing ideas. Careful examination of others' views can lead to the readers' understanding of the logical inconsistencies in their own opinions, perspective on why they hold an opinion, and the consideration of the possibility that their opinion requires further evaluation.

Evaluating Other Opinions

To ensure that this type of examination occurs, Opposing Viewpoints books present all types of opinions. Prominent spokespeople on different sides of each issue as well as well-known professionals from many disciplines challenge the reader. An additional goal of the series is to provide a forum for other, less known, or even unpopular viewpoints. The opinion of an ordinary person who has had to make the decision to cut off life support from a terminally ill relative, for example, may be just as valuable and provide just as much insight as a medical ethicist's professional opinion. The editors have two additional purposes in including these less known views. One, the editors encourage readers to respect others' opinions—even when not enhanced by professional credibility. It is only by reading or listening to and objectively evaluating others' ideas that one can determine whether they are worthy of consideration. Two, the inclusion of such viewpoints encourages the important critical thinking skill of objectively evaluating an author's credentials and bias. This evaluation will illuminate an author's reasons for taking a particular stance on an issue and will aid in readers' evaluation of the author's ideas.

As series editors of the Opposing Viewpoints Series, it is our hope that these books will give readers a deeper understanding of the issues debated and an appreciation of the complexity of even seemingly simple issues when good and honest people disagree. This awareness is particularly important in a democratic society such as ours in which people enter into public debate to determine the common good.

Those with whom one disagrees should not be regarded as enemies but rather as people whose views deserve careful examination and may shed light on one's own.

Thomas Jefferson once said that "difference of opinion leads to inquiry, and inquiry to truth." Jefferson, a broadly educated man, argued that "if a nation expects to be ignorant and free . . . it expects what never was and never will be." As individuals and as a nation, it is imperative that we consider the opinions of others and examine them with skill and discernment. The Opposing Viewpoints Series is intended to help readers achieve this goal.

David L. Bender & Bruno Leone,
Series Editors

Greenhaven Press anthologies primarily consist of previously published material taken from a variety of sources, including periodicals, books, scholarly journals, newspapers, government documents, and position papers from private and public organizations. These original sources are often edited for length and to ensure their accessibility for a young adult audience. The anthology editors also change the original titles of these works in order to clearly present the main thesis of each viewpoint and to explicitly indicate the opinion presented in the viewpoint. These alterations are made in consideration of both the reading and comprehension levels of a young adult audience. Every effort is made to ensure that Greenhaven Press accurately reflects the original intent of the authors included in this anthology.

Introduction

"Teenage decisions about sexuality are influenced by complex, intertwined factors such as love, substance abuse, poverty, family, sexual abuse, racism and religion."
— Photojournalist Dan Habib in his 1995 traveling lecture, "Teen Sexuality in a Culture of Confusion" ·

Sex is a pervasive theme in American culture. Television commercials regularly show sexualized images of men's and women's bodies with the implication that these sexy and desirable people will fulfill the viewers' fantasies. Plots involving sexual pursuit and gratification are staples on television and in the movies. Music videos of all types emphasize sexual situations often with explicit language and imagery. These pop culture representations portray sex as casual, guilt-free, and the ultimate goal of every date or relationship. Teens—and adults—who continually see these portrayals of sexual encounters may come to believe that engaging in promiscuous and premarital sex is normal and expected behavior. The National Campaign to Prevent Teen Pregnancy quotes one teen's view of sex in its 1999 report on teen pregnancy:

> I think the media can influence a lot of younger kids who don't know [about sex]. They think that [how sex is depicted on TV and in the movies] is how it's going to be: You come home after the first date, you have sex with someone, and it's all glamorous, and that's it. They think because they see their favorite movie stars doing it, . . . they can just follow them.

Teens who accept the media's portrayal of sex as fun, glamorous, and a rite of passage to adulthood are often surprised when their own sexual experiences do not live up to their expectations. The Hollywood version of sex shows people meeting, having sex, falling in love, and living happily ever after. Rarely does the media show any of the negative consequences of sexual activity—pregnancy, sexually transmitted diseases, disillusionment, or broken hearts, for example. Maturity and life experiences can prepare some teens for some of the consequences of sexual activity and lessen the effect of others, yet many teens are unprepared for their feelings of regret or emptiness after sex. Shauna, who was eighteen years old when she first had sex with her boyfriend, explains how emotionally lost she felt after the experience:

> Instead of feeling like I'd crossed some sacred threshold into true womanhood, I felt like I'd just slammed the door on ever being a little girl again. I was 18—an adult by legal standards—and yet there was still a little girl inside of me who wasn't quite ready to let go of who she was. I felt as if I'd given away a part of me that I could never get back.
>
> I think I assumed too much. I thought that since my partner loved me a great deal and we'd given the event so much forethought, I would be left with a rosy "afterglow" instead of the emptiness I felt.

According to Shauna, Hollywood's portrayal of premarital sex is "The Big Lie."

Many parents, teachers, and religious and political leaders agree with Shauna's view that movies and television send teens the wrong message when it comes to sex. Many adults (and more and more teens) believe that sexual intercourse forms the most intimate bond between a man and woman and is therefore immoral outside of marriage. Parents worry that media portrayals of sex will override the moral and religious beliefs they have tried to instill in their children and influence them to have sex before they are emotionally ready. In response to many parents' concerns, Congress decreed in its 1996 Welfare Reform Act that school-based sex education programs should teach that "a mutually faithful monogamous relationship in the context of marriage is the expected standard of human sexual activity" and that "sexual activity outside of marriage is likely to have harmful psychological and physical effects."

But new studies show that teens may be paying more attention to their parents' values than was previously thought. In 1998, the Centers for Disease Control and Prevention (CDC) reported that the teen sex rate had dropped for the first time during the 1990s. Its 1997 survey of more than sixteen thousand teens found that 48 percent of them had had sexual intercourse, compared with 54 percent in 1991. Defenders of traditional sex education programs point to these statistics and argue that Congress's proposed changes to sex education are unnecessary. However, a second study by Michael Resnick of the University of Minnesota provides another explanation for the drop in teen sexual activity. According to Resnick, parents who spend time with their children and make their values clear are more likely to have children who forgo sex, drugs, alcohol, tobacco, and violence. "It's more than the physical presence of parents, the number of hours a day they're in the home," Resnick contends. "It's their emotional availability." He asserts that teens take note of what is expected of them when their parents make themselves available to their children and express their feelings and values. "The power and the importance of parents continue to persist, even into late adolescence," he maintains.

Parents and other adults have a difficult time fighting the images of free and easy sex that permeate popular culture. Parents want their children to abstain from sex, while teens continually receive the message that sex is fun and a rite of passage into adulthood. And adults' efforts to deal with the problem of teen sex are often controversial. For example, some adults believe that if teens are going to have sex, then they should at least protect themselves and their partners by using contraception, especially a condom. Others believe that promoting contraception encourages teens to have sex. These conflicting views of teen sex are just some of the topics debated by authors in the following chapters: What Factors Influence Teen Attitudes Toward Sex? Should Society Be Concerned About Teen Sex? How Should Society Respond to Teen Sex? and What Should Teens Be Taught About Sex? The issue of teen sex is complex and holds critical consequences for both the teens involved and society.

CHAPTER 1

What Factors Influence Teen Attitudes Toward Sex?

Chapter Preface

When the AIDS epidemic was recognized as a serious crisis that threatened the lives of the nation's teenagers, some schools began offering free condoms to students to encourage them to protect themselves against the deadly virus and other sexually transmitted diseases. Many parents, religious and political leaders, and conservatives are adamantly opposed to the practice of giving condoms to students, however. They believe that students should be sexually abstinent until marriage; providing teens with condoms sends a message that adults do not really expect teens to remain abstinent, they argue. Gracie Hsu, a policy analyst with the Family Research Council, contends that not only do school-based contraceptive programs like the condom giveaway fail to reduce teen pregnancy and STDs, "but they are actually associated with an increase in sexual activity among participants."

However, several studies published in 1997 and 1998 found no such association. Comparing thousands of students, researchers found that teens who attended schools that provided free condoms were no more sexually active than teens whose schools did not provide condoms. The rate of sexual activity for both sets of teens was about 50 percent. According to Mark Schuster, author of one of the studies, "The big change was that the [sexually active] boys were more likely to be using condoms, and virgins were much more likely to plan to use condoms when they have their first vaginal intercourse."

The availability of condoms in school is just one of the social and cultural factors that observers believe may affect teen sexual behavior. The authors in the following chapter examine other influences that are thought to sway teen attitudes toward sex.

> *"Parents are a remarkably effective antipregnancy program. The greater the closeness of parent and child, the lower the pregnancy rate."*

Parents Influence Teen Attitudes Toward Sex

Ellen Goodman

In the following viewpoint, syndicated columnist Ellen Goodman reports on a study that found that parents have an important effect on whether their teenage children are sexually active. Teens who have a close relationship with their parents have a lower rate of teen sex and teen pregnancy, according to the study. Goodman encourages parents to talk with their children about sex and values, noting that talking to them about sex does not encourage them to be sexually active.

As you read, consider the following questions:

1. By what percentage had the teen pregnancy rate declined since 1993, as cited by Goodman?
2. According to researchers, is abstinence-only education or better use of contraception responsible for the drop in birthrates?
3. What is the first tip for parents who want to help their children avoid teen pregnancy, as cited by the author?

Reprinted with permission from "Why Teen Pregnancy Is Down," by Ellen Goodman, *The Boston Globe*, May 24, 1998. Copyright ©1998 by The Boston Globe Newspaper Co./Washington Post Writer's Group.

When the news broke in May 1998 that teenage motherhood had dropped by nearly 12 percent in the last five years, I had a bit of trouble putting on my party face.

Teenage motherhood was down to the level of the 1980s? Teenage motherhood was down to the highest level of any industrialized country? Been up so long this looks like down to us?

Nevertheless, the usual suspects claimed credit for the usual reasons. One side said that abstinence education was working. The other side said that contraception was working.

The researchers, meanwhile, said that what's driving the drop in birthrates is not one or the other but both: better use of contraceptives and less sexual activity.

I don't believe in looking a gift statistic in the mouth. But nearly lost in the news cycle was a second piece of research released the same day by the nonpartisan National Campaign to Prevent Teen Pregnancy. This one deserves a rare moment of news recycle.

Parents Matter

The study portrayed the shadowy figures who may in the end make a much bigger difference in lowering teenage pregnancy than condoms or pledges: parents.

For a long time, parents of teenagers have been cast as the beleaguered, hapless characters whose voices are barely heard and rarely respected in a cacophony of peers, pop culture, and body piercers. Mothers and fathers, we are told, are road kill on the way to adulthood.

But the study went through all the research on the role parents play in the teenagers' lives and what impact they have on their children's sexual activity. It turns out that parents are a remarkably effective antipregnancy program. The greater the closeness of parent and child, the lower the pregnancy rate.

As Isabel Sawhill, the president of the National Campaign, puts it succinctly, "When teens have a reasonably close relationship to their parents and when the parents communicate their own values to the children, rates of sexual activity and pregnancy are lower."

This does not mean that a sweaty-palmed 45-minute lecture is better than a thousand condoms. Rather, says the campaign's director, Sarah Brown, "parents who communicate values . . . firmly over a long time in the context of a close relationship can reduce sexual risk. What isn't helpful is no opinion and no conversation."

In the wake of this report, the Campaign has put together "Ten Tips for Parents to Help their Children Avoid Teen Pregnancy." This sounds sort of cutely simplistic until you encounter Tip One: "Be clear about your own sexual values."

This, in fact, has been the sticking point for a whole lot of parents who may still find themselves tongue-tied, or even panicked, about the first question on their kids' agenda: What did you do, Dad? The baby-boom generation of parents was not famous for crystal clarity about sex.

But in reviewing polls and studies, it turns out that parents really have arrived at a consensus about what they want for their kids. They want their teens to postpone sex at least through high school—an age that mysteriously coincides with when they'll be leaving home. And they think birth control needs to be there as a backup.

In other words, parents want to communicate precisely the ideas that seem to be—slowly—working.

Tips for Parents

Sawhill says as well that parents should be less worried about giving mixed messages—kids can understand ambivalence better than hypocrisy—than about giving no messages. One thing the research has shown clearly: Talking with kids about sex does not encourage them to be sexually active.

The other "tips" run from discouraging steady dating before 16 to helping teens have options "for a future that are more attractive than early pregnancy and parenthood." Sometimes easier said than done. But saying is a kind of doing.

"We are trying to break through the notion that parents have no role. It's not true. Parents matter, and teens want to hear from them," says Brown.

Indeed, the argument about teen pregnancy has been stuck for years in a pitched battle over contraceptives or abstinence-only programs. It's been a battle waged in schools and legislatures.

But if any public issue has a private face, it's this one. The most effective "program" may be right on the tip—or the 10 tips—of your tongue.

"Although a few young women brag about their sexual conquests and skills, many simply make themselves available, in part because it seems that everyone else is doing it."

Peer Pressure Influences Teen Attitudes Toward Sex

Kristin Luker

In the following viewpoint, Kristin Luker argues that many teen girls who have had sex did not make a conscious decision about how and when they would lose their virginity. Teens believe sexual activity is common and widespread, she maintains, and girls often feel pressured by their friends to have sex. According to Luker, some girls have sex because they are curious and feel that they are missing out on an experience, while for others, sex is something that "just happened" without being planned. Luker is a professor of sociology and law at the University of California, Berkeley.

As you read, consider the following questions:
1. How do many teen girls describe their first sexual encounter, according to the author?
2. How do boys regard sexual activity, in Luker's view?
3. In Luker's opinion, why is the argument that contraception is responsible for the increase in teen sexual activity misguided?

Excerpted from *Dubious Concepts: The Politics of Teenage Pregnancy*, by Kristin Luker. Copyright ©1996 by the President and Fellows of Harvard College. Reprinted with permission from Harvard University Press, Cambridge, MA.

The sexual revolution has transformed Americans' values, attitudes, and behavior in ways that are unlikely to be reversed. How do teens—should teens—think and act in this new world, and reconcile its alluring promises with its hard realities? How can they manage the consequences of their sexual freedom?

Working Against the Tide

Many people of all political persuasions think that teenagers should simply stop having sex. Liberals argue that public campaigns have induced teenagers to curtail their drug use and that such campaigns could likewise induce them to abstain from sex; conservatives plead for "a little virginity."[1] Unfortunately, both groups are working against the historical tide. Premarital sexual activity has become steadily more common in the twentieth century, throughout the industrialized world. But the sexual revolution has not been fully integrated into people's lives, especially the lives of teenagers. The American public is still unsure whether the tide can or should be turned back. Given society's deep ambivalence about sexual activity among teenagers, young women often find themselves in a state of confusion—a state that is often apparent in the ethnographic accounts. They tell researchers about their decisions concerning sex, contraception, and pregnancy. But when we say that teens "decide" on a course of action in such matters, we may be using much too active a verb. On the one hand, young people are told to "just say no"; on the other, their friends, the media, and society at large foster the idea that sexual activity among teenagers is widespread and increasingly commonplace. If a young woman doesn't want to have sex, she has little in the way of support, since sexual activity has come to be expected.

> They looked at a virgin as being something shameful. They were the type of people who would always tell what happened if they made out with a boy or a boy made out with them. I was the only one they never heard from. They would say, "You don't know what you're missing." The more they talked, the more curious I got. (Theresa, eighteen, black, Washington, D.C.)[2]

> All of my friends were having sex and I was curious to see what it was all about. I didn't even know the guy very well

and I don't even want to know him. It wasn't like it is shown on TV or in the movies. I didn't even enjoy it. (Young woman from Colorado)[3]

All my friends were doing it and they dared me. After all, I was seventeen and had never had sex. I thought maybe I really was missing something. (I wasn't.)[4]

Some girls will have sex to get guys to like them. Some girls do it thinking, "Well, I'm going to keep this boyfriend." If I could, I would tell them, "Don't, until you feel they respect and love you. You're too good to be chasing and trying to make someone stay with you." (Robyn, black, Colorado)[5]

The sexuality that young women express in such ethnographic accounts is often curiously passive. Although a few young women brag about their sexual conquests and skills, many simply make themselves available, in part because it seems that everyone else is doing it.

Get It Over With

Even as they feel pressure to be sexually active, teens are urged to abstain, or at least to "be careful" and use contraceptives. Thus, in their accounts they describe their first sexual intercourse as an experience remarkably devoid of pleasure. They are anxious, in a hurry to get it over with, eager to cross the Rubicon in a leap before courage fails; or they see it as something that "just happened," without anyone's having made an active decision.

Then he asked me to have sex. I was scared and everything, and it was like, "What am I gonna do?" The first time I told him no and he understood. We watched some TV. And he brought me home. Then a couple of days after that he asked me again, I said okay. I guess I said so because I just wanted to show him I wasn't scared to have sex. I was scared. And he kinda knew I was scared. But I guess I was playing a role. I wanted to show him that I'm not scared. So we had sex . . . and now it's like we don't get along. (Young black woman from Oakland, California)[6]

We was going together for two years and we didn't do anything. I was like "no" and he was scared also. Finally we just—hurry up and get it over with. We just took off our clothes real quick. Just hurry up and get it over with and we both shaking and crying. (High school student in a midwestern city)[7]

I didn't talk to my boyfriend about sex, and he didn't talk to me. One day we were together and started hugging and kissing, then we just did it. (Latisha, fifteen, black, Chicago)[8]

And I used to go home and he would call me on the phone and then we were like that for about a month or so and then we just started to get involved. I don't know, he just asked me and I said sure, if that was what you want to do . . . We just did it to do it and then I just got pregnant. (Sally, fifteen, white)[9]

He was someone to lean on. When I was depressed, I figured, I'll lean on him. Next thing you know, I figured I started to listen to him. Then I saw him as more of a friend. Then why not kiss him? Why not touch him? It seemed that one thing led to another. Afterward we never made a big deal out of it like, "Wow, wasn't that great last night." We never even talked much about it . . . We said we shouldn't have let that happen. It won't happen again. And then it did happen again. (Ivy, seventeen, black, Boston)[10]

Little Guidance Is Available

Not only are many young women confused and indecisive when it comes to their first sexual encounters, but they often know few adults whom they can comfortably ask for guidance. According to their own accounts, even their mothers offer little or no help:

Only thing she said was, "Don't be out here messing with no boys." And that was it. (Sherita, twelve, black, Washington, D.C.)[11]

I love my mother, but she never really talked to me, and I don't feel like I can talk to her about private matters. She acts like we shouldn't talk about sex. She only told me after my period, that I shouldn't go with boys. (Latisha, fifteen, black, Chicago)[12]

She didn't want me to know nothing about sex but "just don't do it." But I was like—I was like, gosh, but everybody is doing this and I wanted to try it, too. (Fourteen-year-old, attending high school in a midwestern city)[13]

The little information available on young men shows that they, too, see themselves as failures if they have not had sex. For them, sexual activity is an indication of maturity and masculinity.

If they haven't [had intercourse] then they are like outcasts. Like, "Man, you never made love to a girl!" Some of them

Teens Talk About Peer Pressure

As another school year gets under way, eight Metro Detroit teen-agers who attended a *Detroit News* round-table say students today face pressure from their peers, the media and even adults to try cigarettes, drugs and alcohol. "It's like it's socially acceptable, that's the thing," says Julia Anderson, 15, a sophomore at Plymouth Canton High School.

Students also encounter pressure on other issues—getting good grades; looking good, fitting in; and having sex. . . .

If you graduated high school and hadn't had sex, would you consider yourself unusual or weird?

Anderson: Loser! I think there's more pressure . . . if you're a couple, if you're going out with someone.

Andy Rivard: It's like, 'why haven't you done it yet?'

Anderson: Yeah, it's like 'what—you haven't had sex yet? Come on, get going!'

James Slappy: It wouldn't be yourself perceiving you as a loser, it'd be the other people around you . . .

Erik Green: I might be sheltered but I don't see any of that or hear any of that happening.

So there's a lot of people graduating from high school and they're still virgins?

Andy Ziaja: A lot of people graduate with just their business being their business. . . . I see it as in bad taste for someone to walk around and say, 'I had sex three times this week.'

Susan R. Pollack and Marty Fischhoff, *Detroit News*, September 3, 1998.

---

get teased a lot. It's like on the baseball team and they start talking about that and you have got the younger guys out there and you could tell because they are all quiet and stuff and they won't talk. Some of the other people start laughing at them and start getting on them and get them kind of upset. (Male high school student in a midwestern city)[14]

Premarital sexual activity has become increasingly common in the twentieth century. This is partly due to the fact that people are getting married later, but it is also a function of America's transition from a rural, kinship-based society to a modern, industrial one that tends to disconnect sex from marriage. Some experts argue that the real sexual revolution in the United States occurred in the 1880s and was largely over by 1915. Others maintain that there were two sexual revolutions, one between 1915 and 1925 and the other between 1965 and 1975. All agree, however, that sexual activity among teenagers is not peculiar to the late twentieth century; rather, it is the result of long-term trends shaped by social and economic forces that are probably irreversible. Furthermore, whatever it is about modernity that makes sex independent from marriage, it is present in most of the industrialized nations. Teens all over the developed world are engaging in sex before marriage. When in 1984 the United Nations undertook a survey of adolescent sexual and reproductive behavior, it concluded that "without doubt, the proportion of teenagers who have experienced sex by age nineteen has been increasing steadily over the years among all adolescents."[15] Even conservative Japan—a communitarian society with strongly internalized social controls—has reported increases in sexual activity among its teenagers, as well as a rise in out-of-wedlock childbearing. Surveys conducted by the Japanese government in 1981 found that in Japan about 28 percent of young women and 37 percent of young men were sexually active by the end of their teenage years—figures that were less than half of those for the United States but that, compared with the proportions in 1974, represented an increase of 40 percent for young men and an amazing 150 percent for young women.

Contraception's Effect on Teen Sex

According to conservatives, the fact that contraception was made available to teenagers in the late 1960s was the fuel that ignited the explosion of early sex. Prior to 1964 contraceptives were nominally illegal in many jurisdictions, were never mentioned in public (much less advertised), and were difficult to obtain. In pharmacies, condoms were typically kept behind the counter, and some pharmacists in small towns refused to sell them to young men they knew to be unmarried. Since out-of-wedlock pregnancy was stigmatized and likely to lead to a clandestine abortion or a hasty marriage, there is a certain logic to the notion that the stunning reversal in the status of contraception—from illegal and unmentionable to widely available at public expense—fostered the spectacular increase in sexual activity among teenagers.

And since this increase in activity and the proliferation of low-cost birth control clinics both occurred in the late 1960s and early 1970s, there is at least a temporal connection between the two.

Problems

This commonsensical and comforting notion (comforting because it implies that one way to curtail sexual activity among teens is to limit the availability of contraception) has several things wrong with it. First, a great many aspects of American society were changing in the sixties and seventies. Public attitudes shifted radically on issues such as contraception, premarital sex, abortion, and illegitimacy; family planning clinics were only one part of the context surrounding teenagers' behavior. Second, as we have seen, young people throughout the industrialized world have increased their premarital sexual activity, despite the fact that policies regarding contraception vary widely from country to country. Finally, and perhaps most tellingly, in the 1980s federal funding of family planning services dropped sharply—from $400 million in 1980 to $250 million in 1990—but sexual activity among teens continued to increase. The states compensated in some measure for the cutbacks, but they by no means filled the gap entirely. Though it is disappointing not to be able to pinpoint a cause for the increase in sexual activity among the young, historical and international evidence suggests that it is probably the result of a blend of factors. What *is* extremely clear is that the welter of societal changes and conflicting messages surrounding sexual activity has left many young people confused, misinformed, and adrift.

Footnotes

1. The plea for "a little virginity" was made in a full-page advertisement purchased by the conservative advocacy group Focus on the Family. The ad, which appeared in 1991 and 1992, ran in newspapers nationwide, including the *Los Angeles Times*, the *New York Times*, the *Chicago Tribune*, the *Wichita Eagle*, and the *St. Louis Post-Dispatch*.

2. Leon Dash, *When Children Want Children: The Urban Crisis of Teenage Childbearing* (New York: William Morrow, 1989), pp. 124–25.

3. Donna Ewy and Rodger Ewy, *Teen Pregnancy—The Challenges We Faced, The Choices We Made: Teens Talk to Teens About What It's Really Like to Have a Baby* (New York: Signet, 1984), p. 243.

4. Ibid., p. 243.

5. Ibid., p. 251.

6. Elaine Kaplan, "The Lure of Motherhood" (Diss., University of California at Berkeley, 1988).

7. Katharine G. Herr, "An Ethnographic Study of Adolescent Pregnancy in an Urban High School" (Diss., Ohio State University, 1988), p. 146.

8. Mary S. Nelums, "Antecedents to Teenage Pregnancy" (Diss., University of Illinois at Chicago, 1989), p. 63.

9. Jill Taylor, "Development of Self, Moral Voice, and the Meaning of Adolescent Motherhood" (Diss., Harvard University, 1989), p. 84.

10. Constance Willard Williams, "An Acceptable Life: Pregnancy and Childbearing from the Black Teen Mother's Perspective" (Diss., Brandeis University, 1989), p. 99.

11. Dash, *When Children Want Children*, p. 68.

12. Nelums, "Antecedents to Teenage Pregnancy," p. 63.

13. Herr, "An Ethnographic Study," p. 127.

14. Ibid., p. 154.

15. United Nations, Department of International Economic and Social Affairs, "Adolescent Reproductive Behavior: Evidence from Developed Countries," *Population Studies* 1, no. 109 (1988): 49.

"The overwhelming impression that television gives about sex is positive. Seldom are the negative consequences of sex portrayed."

Television Influences Teen Attitudes Toward Sex

William Beaver

Illegitimacy is a serious problem in the United States and is responsible for many of society's ills, argues William Beaver in the following viewpoint. He contends that television is a major contributor to the problem of illegitimacy because of its significant impact on the developing values of children. Explicit sex, sex talk, and innuendo are aired on television at hours when children are listening and watching, he asserts. Children absorb and imitate the sexual messages they receive, he maintains, and because the consequences of sex are rarely portrayed on television, the out-of-wedlock pregnancy rate is soaring. Beaver is a professor of education and social sciences at Robert Morris College in Pittsburgh, Pennsylvania.

As you read, consider the following questions:
1. According to Beaver, what percentage of children are born to single mothers, and what is the illegitimacy rate expected to climb to by 2000?
2. How many hours per week does the typical child spend watching television, as cited by the author?
3. Why must illegitimacy be linked with television viewing, according to Christopher Jencks?

Excerpted from "Illegitimacy and Television," by William Beaver, *Journal of Social, Political, and Economic Studies*, Spring 1996. Reprinted with permission.

The disturbing statistics about illegitimacy in the United States have become all too familiar. Out-of-wedlock births have increased by 200 per cent during the past three decades, to the point that 33 per cent of the children born in this country are to single mothers, usually in their late teens or early twenties. Some predict that by the year 2000 the figure will climb to 40 per cent. Even more disturbing is the impact that single parenthood appears to have on children. For example, a child raised by an unmarried mother compared to one raised in an intact family is six times more likely to live in poverty, three times more likely to be expelled from school, twice as likely to drop out of high school, and three times more likely to suffer emotional problems. Another study conducted by the National Center for Juvenile Justice revealed that 56 per cent of the juveniles in correctional facilities came from single parent homes. For intact families the figure was 28 per cent. In short, some of America's most troubling social problems are associated with out-of-wedlock births—regardless of the debate as to the extent to which these are causally dependent on environmental or genetic factors.

The Most Destructive Social Ill

Conservative thinkers have been most prominent in focusing the country's attention on illegitimacy, because they consider it to be the most destructive of all social ills. In fact, Charles Murray doubts that American society can survive if the epidemic of out-of-wedlock births continues. Murray has also pointed out that illegitimacy is no longer confined to the minority community: currently twenty-two per cent of all white births are to single mothers, and that figure is also rising.

To help combat the problem, two specific governmental solutions have been suggested. Foremost among these is the removal of economic incentives believed to encourage single parenthood, specifically the curbing of welfare payments to unwed mothers. In the Fall of 1995, Congress passed legislation that would have prohibited welfare benefits to unwed mothers if they were not living with a parent, relative, or legal guardian. Whether or not such provisions will ever become law in the U.S. remains to be seen, since President Clinton vetoed the legislation. The other proposed measure involves economic support for married couples with children—largely by way of tax breaks. This way of combatting illegitimacy by encouraging marriage seems far more likely to become law, since neither political party wants to be accused of being anti-family.

However, many who are concerned with the problem of illegitimacy feel that ultimately there is little that government can do to solve the problem. Rather, they believe that only a shift away from a sexually-charged culture that debases the sexual behavior of young people will bring about meaningful change. As former Secretary of Education William Bennett put it, "Political solutions are not ultimately the answer to problems that are at root moral and spiritual." The answer, they claim, is to promote a return to what historian Gertrude Himmelfarb has termed "Victorian virtues." These involve a promotion of a sense of individual responsibility, self-restraint, respectability, and temperate behavior. These are perceived as being values which if internalized will guide the behavior of young people away from early and irresponsible sexual experience and the pregnancies that too often result. But how will this happen? Presumably government initiatives might help to send the message that illegitimacy is socially undesirable, and that strong, intact families are not only socially desirable but positively essential to society. Obviously, parents play an essential important role in the transmission of cultural values, but not the sole role by any means. In today's world other agencies, most notably television, play a significant role in the development of children. Hence parents need help from other segments of society.

Children, Television, and Sex

Although much has been made recently of the potentially degrading effects of movies, rap music, and cyberspace, television would seem to have a far more pervasive impact on children. The typical child in the United States spends about twenty-five hours a week watching television. By the time a person has reached the age of eighteen they will have logged about 19,000 hours in front of the tube—more than any other activity except for sleep. Moreover, with parents spending less time with their children (20 per cent less since 1970), television's role in the socialization process has grown. As television researcher Donald R. Anderson of the University of Massachusetts put it in referring to television, "it fills the social gap once taken by parents, grandparents, schools, and church." It also goes without saying that parents have less time to monitor and supervise what their children watch.

A Significant Impact

Although the precise psychological impact of television is still open to question, it would be naive to assume that it is not significant. Any activity practiced so persistently as television-watching is likely to have meaningful effects. A 1988 study sponsored by the U.S. Department of Education concluded that children, far from being turned into zombies, learn much from television, both good and bad. In terms of what they learn that is bad, the most researched subject has been violence, and the emerging conclusion is that television, while not creating copycat violence, does play a role in producing aggression in children. For instance researcher Susan Hearold, after reviewing 230 studies on television violence involving more than 100,000 subjects, concluded that viewing antisocial acts is positively associated with antisocial behavior.

Much less research has been conducted about sex on television and its impacts on young people, but it seems reasonable to assume that something is going on for several reasons. First, consider the amount of sexual messages on television. One study found that there were 10.9 sexual behaviors per hour either physical, verbal, or implied. A study published by Monique Ward of the University of California, Los Angeles (UCLA), focused on the shows most popular among children. The study revealed that on average 29 per cent of the interactions on those shows involved some sort of sexual talk. Perhaps it should not be surprising then that more than one-half the sexual situations and use of crude language occurred during the 8 o'clock family hour. Why so much sex during the so-called family hour? The most obvious answer is competition.

The Fox Network in order to gain a foothold began airing more sexually explicit shows like *Beverly Hills 90210* and *Melrose Place* during the family hour. *Melrose Place* story lines have included voyeurism, bondage, and sadomasochism, in addition to the heavy doses of more normal sexual behaviors. It's little wonder that children's sexual knowledge is far greater than a generation ago.

Reprinted by permission of Chuck Asay and the Creator's Syndicate.

Once these shows gained ratings points the other networks felt compelled to follow suit. So, for example, *Roseanne* was moved into the family hour slot, and even a show like the *Fresh Prince of Bel-Air,* although not displaying overt sexuality, is now heavily laden with sexual innuendo. Of course high sexual content is not limited to prime time. If anything, talk shows, soap operas, and the tabloids are more sexually charged. In fact some critics maintain that these shows are increasingly making prime time look tame. (Approximately one-half the topics on talk shows are of a sexual nature.) So on any given day during the past couple of years kids could have watched Sally Jesse Raphael interview mothers who allow and even encourage their teenage daughters to have sex,

Phil Donahue discussing fantasy dates with Penthouse Pets (with the Pets, of course, on stage), or Hard Copy's exposé on *Charlie Sheen's Porno Queens.* Moreover, these shows are often aired at times that working parents are unable to monitor their child's viewing, even if they wanted to.

The Psychological Effects

Coupled with the sheer volume of sexual messages are the psychological effects involved. A great deal of research, including that conducted by Michael S. LaTour and Richard E. Pitts published in the *Journal of Advertising,* indicates that sex, like violence, gets the viewer's attention along with arousing them. Other research, including the classic studies by Albert Bandura, have shown that children imitate adults. This is particularly true if the character is attractive and rewarded for their actions. Research also has demonstrated that watching others perform acts tends to lower the viewer's own inhibitions. For instance, Dolf Zillmann conducted an experiment in which male and female undergraduates regularly viewed sexually explicit films. After several weeks of exposure Zillman found that his subjects were more accepting of both premarital and extramarital sexual behavior than before the experiment began.

If TV does have these effects then parents have something to worry about. As one TV critic and mother put it, "Kids know that all the teenagers on their favorite shows Do It—the only question is when." Adding to the problem is that portrayals of sexual intercourse on television usually take place between unmarried persons. A 1991 study by the American Family Association found that for every scene depicting sexual intercourse within marriage, 14 showed sex outside of marriage. Plus the fact that the overwhelming impression that television gives about sex is positive. Seldom are the negative consequences of sex portrayed—usually it's glamorized—quite the opposite of what actually occurs when a teenager becomes pregnant.

Finally, psychological conditioning is at work on television, particularly in advertising. Typically a product is paired with some sexual stimuli. The viewer then associates their sexual feelings with the product, which the sponsor hopes will induce the viewer to make a purchase. Unfortunately, with so many sexual messages on television, it's the sex that gets reinforced. In fact, a study conducted by Wayne Alexander and Ben Judd Jr. published in the *Journal of Advertising Research*, found that when advertisements use sexual stimuli, the viewer tends to remember more about the sex than the product itself.

An Important Part of the Mix

What's to be made of all this? Certainly television is not the only factor involved in shaping a young person's sexual values and behavior. Nevertheless, it seems reasonable to assume that television is an important part of the mix when one considers the amount of time young people spend watching television, the volume of sexual messages aired, coupled with the various psychological factors involved. Moreover, Christopher Jencks, in his book *Rethinking Social Policy*, argues that TV and illegitimacy must be linked, simply because other factors cannot explain the rising numbers of middle class teen pregnancies. Factors such as welfare payments and lack of job for males that are used to explain teen pregnancies in the inner cities, are not common to the middle class. . . .

A Ratings System

Perhaps more than any other measure, a rating system will allow parents to make prudent decisions about what their children watch. Presumably ratings will be published in the various television listings, helping parents to determine the appropriateness of a program. Currently about one-half the parents surveyed say they monitor their children's viewing. A rating system will only encourage more parents to pay attention to programming. Polls also indicate that a rating system will be popular. For example, the *USA Today* survey found that 83 per cent of the respondents now favor a rating system.

Besides a ratings system, the new telecommunications bill requires that beginning in 1998 (barring lawsuits) each television set sold in the U.S. must be equipped with a v-chip. The chip would send a signal over the airwaves alerting parents about a particular program's level of violence, sex, and profanity. To do so the chip would interpret a code embedded in the videotape. . . .

The development of a ratings system and the v-chip should give parents more control in determining what shows their children watch. This may help parents to nurture the values that will guide their children away from early sexual activity, but it needs to become more widely recognized that television has become an integral part in the life of a child, and that the sexual content of programs may be promoting social ills. Increasing levels of restraint, along with ratings and the v-chip, should meantime play some role in lessening illegitimacy.

> *"Because of the fear of AIDS . . . oral sex*
> *has become a commonplace initiation into*
> *sexual activity, widely perceived by many*
> *young people as less intimate, and less risky,*
> *than intercourse."*

Fear of AIDS Influences Teen Attitudes Toward Sex

Tamar Lewin

In the following viewpoint, Tamar Lewin, a staff writer for the *New York Times*, reports that teenagers are changing their sexual practices to protect themselves against the AIDS virus. Lewin writes that after being taught for years about the dangers of sexually transmitted diseases and AIDS, teens view vaginal intercourse as a dangerous behavior that requires an emotional commitment. However, much to the alarm of sex educators, teens consider oral sex to be a safe alternative to intercourse—and not as intimate—and do not take precautions against HIV.

As you read, consider the following questions:
1. What percent of teens polled in 1994 had had oral sex, according to a study cited by Lewin?
2. According to the author, how has the media contributed to the casual acceptance of oral sex?
3. What are the generational differences regarding oral sex, as cited by Lewin?

For parents wondering just how much things have changed since the days when they were first experimenting with dating and sex, the answer is right there in the nurse's office at Hunter High School, a New York City public school for gifted students.

On the shelf in the nurse's bathroom is a box of condoms, to help students avoid pregnancy and protect themselves against AIDS and other sexually transmitted diseases.

And right next to it is a box of mint-flavored condoms with no spermicide, labeled "ONLY for oral sex."

A Common Initiation into Sexual Activity

In part because of the fear of AIDS, and in part because of a basic shift in sexual practices, those who study adolescent sexuality say, oral sex has become a commonplace initiation into sexual activity, widely perceived by many young people as less intimate, and less risky, than intercourse. Many girls also see it as a means of avoiding pregnancy and of preserving their virginity.

"Times change, and the norms of adolescent sexual behavior change with them," said Dr. Mark Schuster, a Los Angeles pediatrician and lead author of a study of adolescent sexual practices. "Among adults, oral sex was part of the sexual revolution of the 1960's and 1970's. And in an era when vaginal intercourse is seen as dangerous, especially in major cities where AIDS is more prominent, many adolescents view oral sex as an alternative. This doesn't mean that they don't go on to vaginal intercourse."

Dr. Schuster's study, published in November in the *American Journal of Public Health*, found that even among Los Angeles high school students who were still virgins, 10 percent had engaged in oral sex—and that boys and girls were equally likely to be the receiving partner.

Some health experts say the popularity of oral sex is worrisome because many teen-agers incorrectly believe it is so safe that they need not take precautions against AIDS and other sexually transmitted diseases.

A 1994 study conducted by Roper Starch, a national polling organization, found that 26 percent of a nationally representative sample of high school students had had oral sex, and 4 percent had engaged in anal sex. Among those in the survey who had already had intercourse, two-thirds had also had oral sex. There are little comparative data from past decades, but those who teach and counsel adolescents say they have no question that there has been a significant rise in the prevalence of oral sex, and a decline in the age at which it starts—with little awareness of the health risks.

"It is incredible how casual oral sex has become for some adolescents," said Dr. Carol Perry, who was a psychologist for 15 years at Riverdale Country School and Trinity School, two private schools in New York City, and who is now in private practice. "With older people, it was something that usually came further along in a relationship, when two people had been comfortable with each other and intimate for a while. But many of the adolescents see it as safer than intercourse, and not as intimate."

AIDS Awareness

In part, the change may be due to the awareness of AIDS and other sexually transmitted diseases. In interviews, many young people say that for as long as they can remember, sex education classes have drummed into their heads the idea that intercourse is dangerous, and potentially fatal. And there are signs that that message has gotten through: condom use by younger adolescents is rising.

"This is the first generation for whom AIDS has been part of their life from the moment they were old enough to start school," said Debra Haffner, president of SIECUS, a group promoting sex education. "Most of them started hearing about sex abuse in preschool, getting told that sex is something a stranger can do to hurt you. Then in third grade, they heard about AIDS, that sex can kill you. In about 10th grade, they started learning about date rape, that even someone you thought was nice can use sex to hurt you. It has to add up to some pretty scary attitudes."

But if intercourse is widely perceived as dangerous, oral sex is not.

"For the people I know, sexual intercourse is a humongous thing," said a 15-year-old Manhattan girl who attends a private school. "It's risky, and it's a big deal. But oral sex doesn't seem like sex. People may see the first time as a rite of passage, but after that, it's nothing much. A friend told me she'd done it to a boy last weekend, and I didn't even think to ask if she'd used a condom. But if she were having intercourse, I'd make her promise me that she would protect herself."

Boys, too, perceive a fundamental difference between intercourse and oral sex. "Everybody understands that intercourse is dangerous and that it requires a real commitment," said a 14-year-old boy, adding that oral sex did not necessarily imply a real relationship.

Many of those interviewed—teen-agers and sex educators alike—say that the casual acceptance of oral sex comes in good part from the media, especially movies like "Pretty Woman," in which Julia Roberts portrayed a prostitute who would perform oral sex with clients, but would not kiss them, because kissing was too intimate.

Few Precautions Taken

And few of them say they know of anyone who has used a condom for oral sex. Counselors and sex-education teachers say that although they make a point of telling adolescents that AIDS and other sexually transmitted diseases can be contracted through oral sex, especially by those with open sores in their mouth or recent dental work, students do not seem to be taking their advice to use condoms or dental dams. For that matter, they say, precautions in oral sex still seem to be unusual among adults, as well.

"When I was at Trinity and I was going to talk about dental dams, I went to the drugstores in the area to see if they were available, and they weren't," Dr. Perry said. "Most of them directed me to the toothbrush section. So I took latex condoms and showed how to cut them to make a dental dam. But this is not something I think most kids, or most adults, are really doing."

It was mostly to prod students to think about the risks of oral sex that the nurse at Hunter began offering the mint condoms in January.

The mint condoms are now being taken at a faster clip than the regular ones. Elaine Sarfati, the school nurse, said she restocks 20 or 30 flavored condoms a day to the box on the shelf in the bathroom of her office—a shelf high enough to be out of the way of younger children.

"In talking with kids, I found that a lot of them didn't think oral sex was sex," Ms. Sarfati said. "They think of it as a safe way of being close."

Less Sex, Safer Sex

Fewer teens are engaging in risky sexual behavior. The trend from 1991 to 1997:

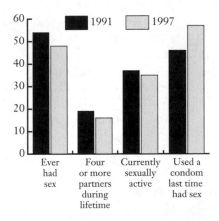

Centers for Disease Control and Prevention, *MMWR*, September 18, 1998.

And though few young people begin to experiment with it before high school, sex educators say, most urban children know about oral sex by the age of 10 or 11.

"Questions about oral sex start in fifth or sixth grade, not because kids are doing it, but because they've heard about it and they're curious," said Dr. Cydelle Berlin, the health educator who founded the Adolescent AIDS prevention program at Mount Sinai Medical Center. "By seventh grade, they want to know if it's really safer sex, and what are the mechanics. For girls, 'Do you spit or do you swallow?' is a typical seventh-grade question. Most parents would be shocked at what their kids know, and what they want to know. I talk to parents' groups sometimes, and they're shocked, surprised, trembling."

Generational Differences

Oral sex has not always been part of most Americans' sexual repertoire. According to a 1994 study of American sexual practices, only a minority of women over 50 had ever performed oral sex. Among women younger than 35, however, more than three-quarters had done so. Most men, whatever their age, had been both givers and receivers of oral sex.

"There are a lot of generational and cultural differences in attitudes to sex," said Dr. Berlin, whose programs reach thousands of adolescents each year, at Mt. Sinai's adolescent clinic and at public and private schools. "But especially among white middle-class adolescents, the acceptance of oral sex as a less risky activity is more widespread than it used to be."

Many educators say that after years of hearing about the perils of AIDS, their students perceive oral sex as a responsible expression of sexuality.

"With all the AIDS education they've had, kids certainly see sex as dangerous," said Phil Kassen, the middle school principal at the Little Red School House in New York City, and the author of a comprehensive sexuality curriculum. "And no matter what we tell them, they see oral sex as not as dangerous. Given the issues of adolescence, there are also a lot of adolescents who think the adults who talk to them about AIDS are trying to use it as a club to scare them out of having sex. And of course there probably are some adults using it that way."

He and others worry that sex-education programs that focus entirely on AIDS and abstinence do little to help young people learn responsible sexual decision-making. Teaching young people the facts about sexually transmitted diseases, they say, does little to change their behavior.

"If you do a program for 40 minutes, it may increase their knowledge about sex, but it's not going to help them negotiate their sexual behavior," Dr. Perry said. "Adolescents are having sex earlier, and they know more, but even kids who can rattle off the facts get very awkward when they have to talk about negotiating safe sex or contraception. It's important for them to understand that if you can't really talk to your partner, you're not ready to engage in something that is a very mature act."

> *"Often dating encourages intimacy for the
> sake of intimacy—two people getting close
> to each other without any real intention of
> making a long-term commitment."*

Dating Influences Teen Attitudes Toward Sex

Joshua Harris

In the following viewpoint, Joshua Harris argues that dating encourages short-term, uncommitted relationships that are based on physical attraction. Dating also tends to skip the friendship stage of a relationship, he contends, and moves right on to intimacy. Furthermore, Harris maintains, dating couples often concentrate on the physical aspect of their relationship, mistaking lust for love. Because sexual expressions of affection are a gift from God, dating—and the feelings of romantic love and intimacy that accompany it—should be reserved for marriage, he asserts. Harris is the author of *I Kissed Dating Goodbye*, from which the following viewpoint is excerpted.

As you read, consider the following questions:
1. According to Harris, what is the point of most dating relationships?
2. Why is the friendship stage of a relationship important, in the author's opinion?
3. How does dating substitute sex for love, according to Harris?

When I was a kid, my mom taught me two rules of grocery shopping. First, never shop when you're hungry—everything will look good and you'll spend too much money. And second, make sure to pick a good cart.

I've got the first rule down, but I haven't had much success with that second rule. I seem to have a knack for picking rusty grocery carts that make clattering noises or ones with squeaky wheels that grate on your nerves like fingernails on a chalkboard.

The "Swerver"

But by far the worst kind of cart you could pick is the "swerver." Have you ever dealt with one of these? This kind of cart has a mind of its own. You want to go in a straight line, but the cart wants to swerve to the left and take out the cat food display. (And, much to our dismay and embarrassment, it too often succeeds!) The shopper who has chosen a swerving cart can have no peace. Every maneuver, from turning down the cereal aisle to gliding alongside the meat section, becomes a battle—the shopper's will pitted against the cart's.

Why am I talking to you about shopping carts when this book is about dating? Well, I recall my bad luck with grocery carts because many times I've experienced a similar "battle of wills" with dating. I'm not talking about conflicts between me and the girls I've dated. I mean that I've struggled with the whole process. And based on my experiences and my exploration of God's Word, I've concluded that for Christians dating is a swerver—a set of values and attitudes that wants to go in a direction different from the one God has mapped out for us. Let me tell you why. . . .

Defective Dating

Dating has built-in problems, and if we continue to date according to the system as it is today, we'll more than likely swerve into trouble. . . .

Dating leads to intimacy but not necessarily to commitment. Jayme was a junior in high school; her boyfriend, Troy, was a senior. Troy was everything Jayme ever wanted in a guy, and for eight months they were inseparable. But two months before Troy left for college, he abruptly announced that he didn't want to see Jayme anymore.

"When we broke up it was definitely the toughest thing that's ever happened to me," Jayme told me afterward. Even though they'd never physically gone beyond a kiss, Jayme had completely given her heart and emotions to Troy. Troy had enjoyed the intimacy while it served his needs but then rejected her when he was ready to move on.

Does Jayme's story sound familiar to you? Perhaps you've heard something similar from a friend, or maybe you've experienced it yourself. Like many dating relationships, Jayme and Troy's became intimate with little or no thought about commitment or how either of them would be affected when it ended. We can blame Troy for being a jerk, but let's ask ourselves a question. What's really the point of most dating relationships? Often dating encourages intimacy for the sake of intimacy—two people getting close to each other without any real intention of making a long-term commitment.

Deepening intimacy without defining a level of commitment is plainly dangerous. It's like going mountain climbing with a partner who isn't sure that she wants the responsibility of holding your rope. When you've climbed two thousand feet up a mountain face, you don't want to have a conversation about how she feels "tied down" by your relationship. In the same way, many people experience deep hurt when they open themselves up emotionally and physically only to be abandoned by others who proclaim they're not ready for "serious commitment."

Icing on the Cake

An intimate relationship is a beautiful experience that God wants us to enjoy. But He has made the fulfillment of intimacy a byproduct of commitment-based love. You might say that intimacy between a man and a woman is the icing on the cake of a relationship headed toward marriage. And if we look at intimacy that way, then most dating relationships are pure icing. They usually lack a purpose or clear destination. In most cases, especially in high school, dating is short term, serving the needs of the moment. People date because they want to enjoy the emotional and even physical benefits of intimacy without the responsibility of real commitment.

In fact, that's what the original revolution of dating was all about. Dating hasn't been around forever. As I see it, dating is a product of our entertainment-driven, "disposable-everything" American culture. Long before *Seventeen* magazine ever gave teenagers tips on dating, people did things very differently.

At the turn of the twentieth century, a guy and girl became romantically involved only if they planned to marry. If a young man spent time at a girl's home, family and friends assumed that he intended to propose to her. But shifting attitudes in culture and the arrival of the automobile brought radical changes. The new "rules" allowed people to indulge in all the thrills of romantic love without having any intention of marriage. Author Beth Bailey documents these changes in a book whose title, *From Front Porch to Backseat*, says everything about the difference in society's attitude when dating became the norm. Love and romance became things people could enjoy solely for their recreational value.

Though much has changed since the 1920s, the tendency of dating relationships to move toward intimacy without commitment remains very much the same.

For Christians this negative swerve is at the root of dating's problems. Intimacy without commitment awakens desires—emotional and physical—that neither person can justly meet. In 1 Thessalonians 4:6 (KJV) the Bible calls this "defrauding," ripping someone off by raising expectations but not delivering on the promise. Pastor Stephen Olford describes defrauding as "arousing a hunger we cannot righteously satisfy"—promising something we cannot or will not provide.

Intimacy without commitment, like icing without cake, can be sweet, but it ends up making us sick.

Skipping the Friendship Stage

Dating tends to skip the "friendship" stage of a relationship. Jack met Libby on a church-sponsored college retreat. Libby was a friendly girl with a reputation for taking her relationship with God seriously. Jack and Libby wound up chatting during a game of volleyball and seemed to really hit it off. Jack wasn't interested in an intense relationship, but he wanted to get to know Libby better. Two days after the retreat he called her up and asked if she'd like to go out to a movie the next weekend. She said yes.

Did Jack make the right move? Well, he did in terms of scoring a date, but if he really wanted to build a friendship, he more than likely struck out. One-on-one dating has the tendency to move a guy and girl beyond friendship and toward romance too quickly.

The Modern Dating Game

As currently practiced, "dating" means a guy and a girl go out together exclusively. It's go steady or nothing. The girl doesn't get to choose whom she'll go out with this weekend and be asked by a different guy next weekend. Instead, once she goes anywhere with "Johnny" (even to the mall to hang out), she is considered "taken" and has lost the option of seeing another guy—unless, of course, there's a big breakup. . . .

In all but a few subcultures, to be dating somebody means to be sleeping together. Kids from Maine to California know that, but parents sometimes find it hard to believe.

Connie Marshner, *Insight*, September 29, 1997.

Have you ever known someone who worried about dating a long-time friend? if you have, you've probably heard that person say something like this: "He asked me out, but I'm just afraid that if we start actually *dating* it will change our friendship." What is this person really saying? People who make statements like that, whether or not they realize it, recognize that dating encourages romantic expectations. In a true friendship you don't feel pressured by knowing you "like" the other person or that he or she "likes" you back. You feel free to be yourself and do things together without spending three hours in front of the mirror, making sure you look perfect.

C.S. Lewis describes friendship as two people walking side by side toward a common goal. Their mutual interest brings them together. Jack skipped this "commonality" stage by asking Libby out on a typical, no-brainer, dinner-and-movie date where their "coupleness" was the focus.

In dating, romantic attraction is often the relationship's cornerstone. The premise of dating is "I'm attracted to you; therefore, let's get to know each other." The premise of friendship, on the other hand, is "We're interested in the same things; let's enjoy these common interests together." If, after developing a friendship, romantic attraction forms, that's an added bonus.

Intimacy without commitment is defrauding. Intimacy without friendship is superficial. A relationship based only on physical attraction and romantic feelings will last only as long as the feelings last.

Lust

Dating often mistakes a physical relationship for love. Dave and Heidi didn't mean to make out with each other on their first date. Really. Dave doesn't have "only one thing on his mind," and Heidi isn't "that kind of girl." It just happened. They had gone to a concert together and afterward watched a video at Heidi's house. During the movie, Heidi made a joke about Dave's attempt at dancing during the concert. He started tickling her. Their playful wrestling suddenly stopped when they found themselves staring into each other's eyes as Dave was leaning over her on the living room floor. They kissed. It was like something out of a movie. It felt so right.

It may have felt right, but the early introduction of physical affection to their relationship added confusion. Dave and Heidi hadn't really gotten to know each other, but suddenly they felt close. As the relationship progressed, they found it difficult to remain objective. Whenever they'd try to evaluate the merits of their relationship, they'd immediately picture the intimacy and passion of their physical relationship. "It's so obvious we love each other," Heidi thought. But did they? Just because lips have met doesn't mean hearts have joined. And just because two bodies are drawn to each other doesn't mean two people are right for each other. A physical relationship doesn't equal love.

When we consider that our culture as a whole regards the words "love" and "sex" as interchangeable, we shouldn't be surprised that many dating relationships mistake physical attraction and sexual intimacy for true love. Sadly, many Christian dating relationships reflect this false mind-set.

When we examine the progression of most relationships, we can clearly see how dating encourages this substitution. First, as we pointed out, dating does not always lead to life-long commitment. For this reason, many dating relationships begin with physical attraction; the underlying attitude is that a person's primary value comes from the way he or she looks and performs as a date. Even before a kiss has been given, the physical, sensual aspect of the relationship has taken priority.

Next, the relationship often steamrolls toward intimacy. Because dating doesn't require commitment, the two people involved allow the needs and passions of the moment to take center stage. The couple doesn't look at each other as possible life partners or weigh the responsibilities of marriage. Instead, they focus on the demands of the present. And with that mind-set, the couple's physical relationship can easily become the focus.

And if a guy and girl skip the friendship stage of their relationship, lust often becomes the common interest that brings the couple together. As a result, they gauge the seriousness of their relationship by the level of their physical involvement. Two people who date each other want to feel that they're special to each other, and they can concretely express this through physical intimacy. They begin to distinguish their "special relationship" through hand holding, kissing, and everything else that follows. For this reason, most people believe that going out with someone means physical involvement.

Focusing on the physical is plainly sinful. God demands sexual purity. And He does this for our own good. Physical involvement can distort two people's perspective of each other and lead to unwise choices. God also knows we'll carry the memories of our past physical involvements into marriage. He doesn't want us to live with guilt and regret.

Physical involvement can make two people feel close. But if many people in dating relationships really examined the focus of their relationships, they'd probably discover that all they have in common is lust. . . .

Old Habits Die Hard

We can't fix many of dating's problems by merely "dating right." I believe that dating has dangerous tendencies that don't go away just because Christians do the steering. And even those Christians who can avoid the major pitfalls of premarital sex and traumatic breakups often spend much of their energy wrestling with temptation.

If you've dated, this probably sounds familiar to you. I think that for too long we've approached relationships using the world's mind-set and values, and if you've tried it, you might agree with me that it just doesn't work. Let's not waste any more time battling the swerving cart of dating. It's time for a new attitude.

> *"In today's sexually overheated environment . . . we want to prevent babies, not sex. So we arrive at the final solution—abortion on demand."*

The Legalization of Abortion Has Influenced Teen Attitudes Toward Sex

Joseph Collison

In the past, teens abstained from sex due to fears about pregnancy and sexually transmitted diseases, asserts Joseph Collison in the following viewpoint. Today, however, more teens are sexually active than ever before, he argues, because they know that if they get pregnant they can get rid of their "mistake" through an abortion. According to Collison, the moral erosion caused by the legalization of abortion is leading to infanticide as teens are taught that babies are a burden that should be avoided at all costs. Collison is the director of the office of Pro-Life Activities for the diocese of Norwich, Connecticut, and chairman of Caring Families Pregnancy Services.

As you read, consider the following questions:
1. Why did Amy and Brian kill their baby after it was born instead of having an abortion beforehand, according to Planned Parenthood as cited by Collison?
2. What is the "pseudo-solution" to teen pregnancy and why has it failed, according to the author?
3. In what ways have children's views toward babies changed, in Collison's opinion?

Can a mother forget her infant, be without tenderness for the child of her womb?

—Isaiah 49:15

It was the lead story on the evening news. Two nice young college students, Amy and Brian, drove from New Jersey to Delaware and rented a motel room. There Amy gave birth to a baby boy. Brian, it was reported, beat the baby to death, stuffed him in a plastic bag, and threw him in a trash container.

The body was found and the parents arrested. Defense attorneys suggested that the baby had "died of suffocation" during birth, although it was reported that an autopsy showed he had been shaken and pummeled to death. Psychiatrists gave reasons why "society" was to blame, and the American Civil Liberties Union (ACLU) weighed in with arguments about "rights." A *New York Times* writer dismissed it all as just an "unfortunate outcome of teenage sexuality." Why didn't Amy and Brian just go to an abortionist and have their baby legally and quietly killed? Because, said the public affairs director of Planned Parenthood, "organized religion" has given abortion "a bad name."

Not an Isolated Case

There were a few other such cases at the time that made for sensational news stories. After Amy and Brian there was Melissa, another teenager from New Jersey, who, it was reported, took time out from her senior prom to go to the ladies' room, where she gave birth, wrapped her baby boy in a plastic bag, threw him in the waste basket, and returned to dance with her date. But the sensation began to fade. When it was reported that another girl did a motel-room birth-and-murder like Amy and Brian's the story got scant coverage. And when two "toilet birth" babies were discovered, one in the toilet of an Atlantic City bus terminal (he survived), another in the toilet of a courthouse on Long Island (he didn't), the media reported them, but only briefly.

California newspapers have carried stories about the bodies of newborns washing ashore with the tide, and about dead babies routinely found in dumpsters and restrooms and by roadsides. They have also reported that San Diego sewer workers have been told to watch for little bodies clogging filters. The *Milwaukee Journal Sentinel* has reported on an attorney who specializes in defending neonaticidal mothers (there is a large number of such cases in Wisconsin). But unless facts surrounding these deaths lend themselves to sensationalizing, few cases make the headlines.

Infanticide is fast becoming commonplace in our society. The official estimate of 250 newborns killed annually by their mothers (sometimes fathers) is almost certainly low.

From Immorality to a Constitutional Right

How quickly we have lost our moral bearings! Thirty years ago all Christian churches condemned abortion as gravely immoral, and civic leaders considered the defense of human life to be their fundamental duty. But in 1973 our Supreme Court Justices found strange penumbras, never before noticed, lurking in the Constitution, and on the basis of these weird emanations, abortion was proclaimed a "constitutional right." Almost overnight, Americans, in their simplistic faith that what is legal cannot be immoral, began to exercise that "right."

In one generation society has come to accept the idea, recently voiced by Deborah Rogow of the International Women's Health Coalition, that the "distinction between abortion and contraception is more an ideological construction than a logical response to client's [sic] needs." Not long ago contraception was widely illegal in America and considered immoral by all churches. Now we yawn at four thousand abortions a day.

And we are rapidly coming to accept infanticide. Note the number of "neonatal discards" in our hospitals, where care is often withheld from handicapped newborns. (The number of infants allowed to live with Down's syndrome has decreased by 90 percent in this generation.)

When the *Roe v. Wade* decision was handed down in 1973, social standards collapsed as America became obsessed with sex. Teenage pregnancy increased and parents became frightened. This was the opportune moment for the "culture of death" to offer its pseudo-solution—sex education.

Of course, common sense and historical sense should have taught us that sex education doesn't work. It sexualizes and stimulates children at an unnaturally early age and substan-

Reprinted by permission of Chuck Asay and the Creator's Syndicate.

tially increases sexual activity. This "solution" caused teenage pregnancies to soar. Within a few years, 40 percent of teenage girls were becoming pregnant. The unhappy results of sex education then enabled the culture of death to seize another opportunity. Contraceptives, especially condoms, were soon being pushed on teenagers "to prevent pregnancy." Like sex education, use of contraceptives further increased pregnancy among teenagers, since their availability increases sexual activity, and they often don't work.

A Dilemma

So America is faced with a dilemma. The Great American Sexual Revolution is to be protected at all costs, but we don't want *our* teenagers having babies. The traditional solution, which worked surprisingly well in the past, was to frighten teenagers. Older readers will remember how youthful ardor could be cooled by the fear of pregnancy and venereal disease. In today's sexually overheated environment, however, we want to prevent babies, not sex. So we arrive at the final solution—abortion on demand. But problems remain: Some girls find they don't want an abortion; some have moral qualms;

some actually want the baby. So again, as in the past, we find it expedient to frighten our children. But this time we demonize the babies.

There was a time when little girls mothered baby dolls. They sang to their "babies," loved them, and learned to be mothers. Today's little girls groom and dress their anatomically grotesque Barbie dolls, and with Barbie and Ken they learn to admire and imitate the synthetic sociopaths who gyrate on MTV. In the past, when little girls grew older, they cared for younger brothers and sisters, or baby-sat young neighbors or cousins. But in a society of one-child families and daycare centers, there are no babies to care for. Most teenagers have little personal experience of babies, and in school they are taught that babies are dreadful burdens.

"The Realities of Parenting"

How is this teaching accomplished? The girls are intentionally tormented by a doll manufactured to model "the realities of parenting." Eight-pound "Baby Mike" is widely used in schools these days to convey the message that while teen sex is okay, babies are not okay. A student is assigned to care for Baby Mike for several days. Mike is programmed to cry for 20 minutes at random intervals (including at night), to record abuse when shaken, and to register neglect if his crying is not attended to.

No one loves Baby Mike. And after completing their Baby Mike assignment, it's easy for children to accept the Planned Parenthood ad campaign aimed at school-age children. "Babies Are Loud, Smelly, and Expensive," the ads blare.

So the message is hammered home: If you happen to get pregnant, *do* get an abortion.

Periodical Bibliography

The following articles have been selected to supplement the diverse views presented in this chapter. Addresses are provided for periodicals not indexed in the *Readers' Guide to Periodical Literature*, the *Alternative Press Index*, the *Social Sciences Index*, or the *Index to Legal Periodicals and Books*.

Raymond Arroyo — "Selling Sex on MTV," *Crisis*, April 1997. Available from PO Box 10559, Riverton, NY 08076-0559.

Michael Bronski — "Fundies Upset About Undies," *Z Magazine*, May 1999.

Margaret B. Carlson — "Here's a Precious Moment, Kid," *Time*, September 22, 1997.

J.J. DeSpain — "Virginity 2000," *'Teen*, February 1998.

Marilyn Gardner — "Hollywood Gets Heat for Being Clueless About Images of Girls," *Christian Science Monitor*, May 16, 1997.

Susan Gilbert — "Youth Study Elevates Family's Role," *New York Times*, September 10, 1997.

Marjorie Heins — "Rejuvenating Free Expression," *Dissent*, Summer 1999.

Anita Manning — "Condom Access Shows No Effect on Teen Sex Rate," *USA Today*, April 14, 1998.

Jane Mauldon and Kristin Luker — "Does Liberalism Cause Sex?" *American Prospect*, Winter 1996. Available from PO Box 383080, Cambridge, MA 02238.

Kristine M. Napier — "Chastity Programs Shatter Sex-Ed Myths," *Policy Review*, May/ June 1997.

New York Times — "The Impact of Condoms in School," October 3, 1997.

Douglass G. Norvell — "Something Queer on Campus," *New American*, November 11, 1996. Available from 770 Westhill Blvd., Appleton, WI 54914.

Lynda Richardson — "Condoms in School Said Not to Affect Teen-Age Sex Rate," *New York Times*, September 30, 1997.

Debra J. Saunders — "Gay-Ed for Tots," *Weekly Standard*, August 19, 1996. Available from 1211 Avenue of the Americas, New York, NY 10036.

Ron Stodghill II — "Where'd You Learn That?" *Time*, June 15, 1998.

CHAPTER 2

Should Society Be Concerned About Teen Sex?

Chapter Preface

A 1995 study by the National Survey of Family Growth scandalized much of the nation and provided fodder for news commentaries when it reported that nearly two-thirds of the sexual partners of teen mothers were twenty years old or older. Commentators, policymakers, and parents began worrying that male sexual predators were exploiting innocent young girls and urged lawmakers to enforce statutory rape laws.

In the midst of the media reports about the sexual exploitation of teen girls by adult men, a few commentators offered a dissenting view. In 1997, R.E. Lieb wrote an opinion piece in the Toronto *Globe and Mail* in which he argued that some teenage girls may be willing, and even enthusiastic, participants in their sexual relationships with adult men. The teenage years are a time of raging hormones, Lieb and others assert, and many teens are anxious to learn about and explore their sexuality. Older men are often more attractive to adolescents, the dissenters maintain, because they are frequently more experienced in sexual matters and have more money to spend. For some girls, a sexual relationship with an older man is simply part of the teen years' reckless and thrill-seeking behavior, they contend.

Lieb's views on adolescent girls and adult men are definitely in the minority, however. Roger Tonkin, a pediatrician in British Columbia, wrote that in his practice he sees many teen girls who have been sexually abused, assaulted, and exploited by older men. He argues that men's behavior cannot be justified by the seemingly willing or consensual participation of teenage girls. Adolescents are simply too young for their consent to sex to be meaningful, he maintains, and some may not "even know they have a right to say 'no' and have that word accepted," he writes.

Society's concern over the willingness of underage girls to engage in sexual relationships with men is just a small part of the debate over teen sex. In the following chapter, the authors examine the extent of sexual exploitation of teen girls by adult men, and whether teen pregnancies are a serious problem.

VIEWPOINT 1

"The odds are stacked against the offspring of adolescent mothers from the moment they enter the world."

Teen Pregnancy Is a Serious Problem

Rebecca A. Maynard

Rebecca A. Maynard is associated with the Robin Hood Foundation, a charitable organization that funds antipoverty programs and schools for children and adolescents. The following viewpoint is an excerpt of its report, *Kids Having Kids*, edited by Maynard. Maynard writes that adolescent pregnancy is a serious problem that adversely affects not just the children born out of wedlock, but their mothers, fathers, and society as well. According to Maynard, illegitimate children are more likely to have difficulties in school, suffer health problems, have fewer job prospects, and end up in jail or prison. In addition, she maintains, their parents face welfare dependency, fewer educational prospects, and lower earnings. Society also pays the price for illegitimacy, she contends, because it is forced to pay the costs associated with teen pregnancy.

As you read, consider the following questions:
1. According to the HOME survey, what is home life like for children born of teen mothers?
2. How much more likely is it that daughters of teen mothers will themselves become teen mothers, as cited by Maynard?
3. What percentage of teen mothers earn a high school diploma by age 30, according to the author?

Excerpted with permission from *Kids Having Kids: A Robin Hood Foundation Special Report on the Costs of Adolescent Childbearing*, 1996, edited by Rebecca Maynard.

The odds are stacked against the offspring of adolescent mothers from the moment they enter the world. As they grow, they are more likely than children of later child-bearers to have health and cognitive disadvantages and to be neglected or abused. The daughters of adolescent mothers are more likely to become adolescent moms themselves, and the sons are more likely to wind up in prison.

Low-Birthweight Babies

When compared to children of mothers age 20 or 21 when they had their first child, the children of adolescents are more likely to be born prematurely and 50 percent more likely to be low-birthweight babies—of less than five and a half pounds. Low birthweight raises the probabilities of a variety of adverse conditions such as infant death, blindness, deafness, chronic respiratory problems, mental retardation, mental illness, and cerebral palsy. In addition, low birth-weight doubles the chance a child will later be diagnosed as having dyslexia, hyperactivity, or another disability. Even after factoring out a variety of related background characteristics, the research indicates that adolescent childbearing and closely linked factors heighten the risk of low birthweight and later problems the children, their parents, and their schools must confront.

As they grow, the children of adolescent moms tend to suffer poorer health than do the children of women who were age 20 or 21 when their first child was born. Therefore, one would also expect them to see the doctor more often than do children of later childbearers. But, perversely, they receive only half the level of medical care and treatment their counterparts receive.

Based on parents' reports of their children's health status, children of later childbearers are much more likely to be in "excellent" health than are the children of adolescent moms: 60 percent of the children of the later childbearers are so rated, versus 38 percent of the children of adolescent mothers. Meanwhile, in his or her first 14 years, the average child of an adolescent mom visits a physician and other medical providers an average of 2.3 times per year, compared with 4.8 times for a child of later childbearers. Early childbearing and closely linked factors—such as motivation, peer group influence, and community context—account for about one third of this large difference.

On average, an adolescent mother consumes $3,700 per year in healthcare for her children. Even though each of her children individually receives substantially less care than children of later childbearers, the typical adolescent mom annually consumes nearly 20 percent more medical care for her children than she would if she delayed childbearing until age 20 or 21 for the very simple reason that she has, on average, more children than her older childbearing counterparts do. . . .

The Homes Where They Live

Children of adolescent moms are much less likely than their peers to grow up in homes with fathers. In addition, the quality of the homes where they live is rated substantially lower than those of the comparison group, even after controlling for various background factors. This conclusion is based upon results of the widely accepted Home Observation for Measurement of the Environment (HOME) survey, which rates homes based on the emotional support and cognitive stimulation provided to children. For example, the survey analyzes the amount and quality of attention children receive from their parents and the degree to which their residences contain books, educational toys, and games.

Children of adolescent moms are two to three times more likely than the children of their older childbearing counterparts to report having run away from home during those years. Five percent of adolescent mothers' children are sufficiently miserable in their homes that they report running away from it sometime between the ages of 12 and 16, compared with only about 2 percent of children born to later childbearers.

Children of adolescent moms are also far more likely to be physically abused, abandoned, or neglected. In a study of Illinois Child Protective Service statistics, which are among the best and most comprehensive in the nation, the scholars found that children of adolescent mothers are more than twice as likely to be the victims of abuse and neglect than are the offspring of 20- to 21-year-old moms.

Illinois logged 109 reports of child abuse per 1,000 children born to adolescent moms and only 50 per 1,000 children in the comparison group of children born to mothers who were 20 or 21. To the extent that researchers were able to factor out the influence of background characteristics, their work shows that adolescent childbearing is a major cause of this huge margin of difference in child-abuse rates. In addition, one of every four times Illinois receives a report that a child of an adolescent mother has been abused, it finds abuse so great it places the child in foster care. . . .

Trouble in School

In school, the children of adolescent moms do much worse than those in the comparison group of later childbearers. They are two to three times less likely to be rated "excellent" by their teachers and 50 percent more likely to repeat a grade. And they perform significantly worse on tests of their cognitive development, even after differences in measurable background factors have been screened out.

The research suggests that performance in school does not improve as children of adolescent mothers age. They are far more likely to drop out than are children born to later childbearers. Only 77 percent of the children of adolescent moms earn their high school diplomas by early adulthood, compared with 89 percent of the comparison group. Although a part of this sizable difference in high school graduation-rates can be explained by background differences, 57 percent of the graduation rate gap is due to adolescent childbearing and closely linked factors.

Adolescent Mothers from One Generation to the Next

When compared with their counterparts born to older childbearers, the daughters of adolescent moms are 83 percent more likely themselves to become mothers before age 18. After controlling for various background factors, adolescent childbearing and closely linked factors account for about 40 percent of this difference in adolescent pregnancy rates. Teen mothers beget teen mothers at a far greater rate than older mothers do, and they are far more likely to pass on their poor life prospects as a birthright. Furthermore, the daughters of teen moms, whether or not they become teen moms themselves, are 50 percent more likely to bear children out of wedlock than the comparison group.

Unproductive Lives

A snapshot of adolescent mothers' children at the age of 24 reveals that roughly 30 percent of them are neither in school nor working nor actively looking for a job. At that point in life, they are 71 percent more likely to be unengaged productively than are peers whose mothers delayed childbearing until their early twenties. Less than half of this "economic activity" gap is attributable to observable background factors. Most of the difference is due to adolescent childbearing and closely linked factors. The research suggests, though it does not spell out directly, that the children of adolescent moms are less likely to attend college and more likely to work in low-skill jobs. For these and other reasons, their long-term earnings potential appears to be significantly lower than that of the comparison group born to later childbearers.

The teen sons of adolescent mothers are 2.7 times more likely to land in prison than the sons of mothers who delayed childbearing until their early twenties. Adolescent childbearing by itself accounts for 19 percent of this difference. By extension, adolescent childbearing in and of itself costs U.S. taxpayers roughly $1 billion each year to build and maintain prisons for the sons of adolescent mothers. In addition to the measurable criminal-justice costs, other, less tangible costs, such as damage to people and property, are associated with criminal activity.

Consequences for Adolescent Mothers

In absolute terms, adolescent mothers face poor life prospects. Seven of 10 will drop out of high school. During their first 13 years of parenthood, adolescent moms earn an average of about $5,600 annually, less than half the poverty level. And adolescent mothers spend much of their young adult years (ages 19 to 30) as single parents. Surprisingly, after accounting for differences in background and closely linked factors such as motivation, adolescent mothers earn only slightly less during the first 12 years of parenthood than they would be expected to earn if they delayed childbearing until age 20 or 21. In contrast, over their young adult lives (ages 19 to 30), they work and earn somewhat more than do their later childbearing counterparts.

Mike Smith. Reprinted by permission of United Feature Syndicate, Inc.

Moreover, although their sources of income differ, adolescent mothers have combined incomes from their own earnings, earnings of spouses, child support, and public assistance comparable to those of the older childbearers, after background and closely linked factors are controlled for. During their first 13 years of parenthood, they have income and medical-care assistance valued at just nearly $19,000 annually, compared with just over $20,000 annually for their later childbearing counterparts. After netting out the effects of background and other factors closely linked to early childbearing, adolescent childbearers fare slightly better than their later childbearing counterparts in terms of their overall economic welfare, having total incomes of nearly $20,000 annually as compared with just over $16,000 for the comparison group.

Although total economic support is not greatly affected by adolescent childbearing itself, this relatively modest level of economic support must feed more mouths than does the income of their counterparts who delay childbearing until age 20 or 21, resulting in greater poverty. Larger family sizes, together with weakened chances of stable marriage, lead to about 50 percent higher rates of welfare dependence among adolescent parents.

The really significant consequences of adolescent child-bearing for the mothers are lower levels of educational attainment, higher rates of single parenthood, larger family sizes, and greater reliance on public assistance. Even after parsing out the effects of background and closely linked factors that can explain some of the observed differences in outcomes between adolescent mothers and their later childbearing counterparts, the research shows that adolescent childbearing itself accounts for a 50 percent lower likelihood of completing high school, 24 percent more children, and 57 percent more time as a single parent during the first 13 years of parenthood.

Dropping Out of High School

Pregnancy and parenting pose major challenges to full-time school attendance. As a result, adolescent mothers drop out at a staggering rate, and those who have already dropped out are less likely to return to school. Only about three of 10 adolescent mothers earn a high school diploma by age 30, compared with nearly 76 percent in the comparison group of women who delay childbearing until age 20 or 21. Controlling for a wide range of background variables, scholars found that adolescent childbearing alone accounts for more than 40 percent of this difference in graduation rates. Looked at another way, adolescent childbearing, at its current rate, is directly responsible for over 30,000 adolescent girls in the U.S. annually not completing high school.

All of the school completion gap will be made up by adolescent mothers earning General Education Development (GED) certificates at higher rates than do their older childbearing counterparts. However, an emerging body of research suggests that, although a GED may enhance the earnings potential of school dropouts, it does not close the entire earnings gap.

Adolescent moms spend nearly five times more of their

young adult years as single parents than do women who have their first child at age 20 or 21—four years versus ten months. The research indicates that adolescent childbearing itself is responsible for half of this difference. These same mothers would have spent an average of only 2.7 years as single parents if they had delayed childbearing until age 20 or 21. Also, children who grow up in the homes of single moms are one and a half to two times more likely to become teen parents themselves than are children who live in two-parent families. . . .

Consequences for the Fathers

Boys are one-third as likely as girls to become adolescent parents, according to recent studies of teen sexuality and childbearing. Each year, fewer than 60,000 boys age 17 and younger father children for the first time. The fathers of children born to adolescent mothers are, on average, two and a half years older than the mom; in one fifth of the cases, they are at least six years older. Recent research also suggests that the incidence of pregnancy among adolescent girls often is the result of sexually predatory behavior of older men. Although the *Kids Having Kids* scholars found that the consequences of adolescent childbearing on both young and older fathers are not as sharp as the effects on mothers and their children, they did discover some impacts, especially on younger dads.

Adolescent dads will finish an average of only 11.3 years of school by the age of 27, compared with nearly 13 years by their counterparts who delay fathering until age 21. After the effects of various background variables are screened out, adolescent childbearing and closely linked factors account for adolescent dads finishing one semester less school than the comparison group of older fathers. In many cases, the semester may be the pivotal one that determines whether a high school senior will graduate or drop out.

By age 27, adolescent fathers earn, on average, $4,732 less annually than the comparison group of men who delay fathering until age 20 or 21. Although just over half of this difference is explained by background factors, the research suggests that an average of $2,181 in lower earnings per year is due to adolescent parenting and closely linked factors. As a consequence, adolescent dads are not as prepared as their comparison-group counterparts to contribute financially to the well-being of their young families or—when they do not live with the mothers—to pay child support.

Over the 18 years following the birth of their first children, the dads of children born to adolescent mothers earn, on average, $10,712 per year (in 1996 dollars), compared with $13,796 for the male partners of delayed childbearers. This means they have about $3,000 less per year at their disposal to help support their children and families. Roughly half of these lower earnings are explained by various background factors.

Little of the increased earnings that would result from delayed childbearing is likely to benefit the adolescent mothers and their children. Benefit can be felt only when the parents live together or the father pays child support, but currently only 19 percent of adolescent mothers wed the fathers of their first child before or shortly after the birth of the child. And earlier research demonstrates that a small fraction of nonresident fathers of children born to adolescent mothers pay child support on any regular basis. Currently, only 15 percent of never-married teen moms are ever awarded child support, and those with orders receive, on average, only one third of the amount originally awarded.

Meanwhile, the *Kids Having Kids* researchers found that fathers who do not marry the adolescent mothers of their children have incomes sufficient for society to expect them to contribute support at a level that would offset as much as 40 to 50 percent of the welfare costs to the adolescent mothers and their families. More rigorous paternity establishment and child-support enforcement could provide gains for children and the rest of society.

Costs of Adolescent Childbearing for the Nation

How much does adolescent childbearing cost the United States? Even the very best data, which were culled, arranged, and analyzed for the purpose of this study, cannot possibly give a complete or precise figure. Still, this study gives the clearest estimates to date. It controls for background factors and, where possible, closely linked factors to isolate the economic costs to the nation and to society caused by adolescent childbearing.

In looking at five important dimensions of the problem, researchers estimate that adolescent childbearing itself costs the taxpayers $6.9 billion each year. The higher public-assistance benefits—welfare and food stamps combined—caused by adolescent childbearing cost the taxpayers $2.2 billion. The increased medical-care expenses cost $1.5 billion. Constructing and maintaining prisons to house the increased number of criminals caused by adolescent childbearing costs about $1 billion each year, and the increased costs of foster care are only slightly less at $.9 billion. Due to the sizable effect of adolescent childbearing on the work patterns of fathers, the United States incurs a nontrivial loss of tax revenue—$1.3 billion annually.

The cost to taxpayers of adolescent childbearing *together with* the other disadvantages faced by adolescent mothers is between $13 billion and nearly $19 billion per year—this is the amount the taxpayers would save if a policy successfully delayed adolescent childbearing *and* successfully addressed these other disadvantages.

Social Costs

Beyond the taxpayer expenses described above, another important consequence of adolescent childbearing is a loss in national productivity. A society using its energy and resources to mitigate the problems caused by teen childbearing is unable to expend those resources for more productive purposes. Based largely on the diversion of its resources toward the increased health care, foster care, and incarceration rates apparently caused by adolescent childbearing, researchers calculated a social cost to the nation of just under $9 billion per year. That figure utilizes the tightest controls for various background factors. When researchers control for a moderate range of background factors, they calculate the social cost of adolescent childbearing at $21 billion per year.

The gross annual cost to society of adolescent childbearing and the entire web of social problems that confront adolescent moms and ultimately lead to the poorer and sometimes devastating outcomes for their kids is calculated to be $29 billion.

*"Although many people worry that
pregnancy among teenagers has attained
'epidemic' proportions, teenage women
right now are having babies at about the
same rate as they have for most of the
twentieth century."*

The Extent of Teen Pregnancy Is Exaggerated

Kristin Luker

The public image of teen mothers exaggerates the actual problem of teen pregnancy, asserts Kristin Luker in the following viewpoint. Teen girls are having babies at the same rate they were during most of the twentieth century, she maintains. The only difference between teens of the 1990s and earlier decades, according to Luker, is that pregnant teens in the 1990s are less likely to get married before the birth and are more likely to raise their babies themselves. In addition, Luker asserts, most unwed mothers are not teenagers but older women, many of whom were married at the time of conception. Luker is the author of *Dubious Conceptions: The Politics of Teenage Pregnancy*, from which this viewpoint is excerpted.

As you read, consider the following questions:

1. What percentage of all babies born to unwed mothers in 1990 were born to whites, according to Luker?
2. What percentage of teen mothers were legal adults when their children were born, as cited by the author?
3. What kinds of teenager are most likely to drop out of school when they become pregnant, in Luker's opinion?

At the Eileen Sullivan Daycare Center, in the sunny play-room for toddlers, young David Winters sits entranced in front of a colorful bead-and-wire toy. His chubby fingers tease the beads up and across the bright red, blue, and green wires, his solemnity lightened by rare and dazzling smiles as he conquers a particularly tricky corner in the game.

Born a month prematurely, David has gone on to flourish at the Sullivan Center after a rocky start. Across the street, in the high school to which the daycare center belongs, David's mother, Michelle Brown, is taking her algebra exam. If all goes well and Michelle gets the B she hopes for, she may well succeed at being the first member of her family to graduate from high school. And if she does, she has every intention of crossing that auditorium stage three months from now, dressed in her graduation robes and holding baby David in her arms.

Troubling Questions

Meanwhile, beyond the walls of the school and the daycare center, Michelle and her baby are at the heart of important and troubling questions that are being asked by people from all walks of life. In the United States, although teenagers give birth to only 12 percent of all babies, they represent about a third of all unmarried mothers. These young mothers are somewhat less likely than older mothers to start prenatal care on time, and are slightly more likely to have low-birthweight babies and complications during pregnancy and childbirth—all of which are factors associated with medical and sometimes developmental problems in their children.

Michelle is not sure she's old enough to get married, though she never considered herself too young to have or to raise David, despite the fact that she was only seventeen when he was born. She did think briefly about having an abortion, but both her mother and grandmother were adamantly opposed; and truth to tell, Michelle was secretly happy they were. Their support, combined with her own experiences and those of many of her friends, makes her sure that she can successfully handle being both a young mother and a student. Being a wife is another story, though.

Michelle's reluctance to marry is strengthened by some harsh economic realities. The father of her baby works full time at McDonald's, but his minimum-wage salary of $684 a month just won't support the three of them. He's a diligent and even desperate worker (he competed against more than a hundred other applicants for his job), and he's been promised a promotion to manager. Even managers don't get medical benefits at McDonald's, however, and David's health still calls for frequent and expensive visits to the pediatrician. Although Michelle squirms under what she sees as the shame attached to welfare, she can't afford to give up the money (and especially the medical services that come with it) in order to marry.

Michelle and David's situation illustrates a host of important questions about age, sex, and marriage. To many people over forty, the idea of pregnant teenagers walking openly down school corridors, not to mention the existence of high school daycare centers, is something that outstrips the imagination. Until the mid-1970s visibly pregnant *married* women, whether students or teachers, were formally banned from school grounds, lest their swelling bellies cross that invisible boundary separating the real world (where sex and pregnancy existed) from the schools (where they did not). The idea that a pregnant *unmarried* woman would show herself not only in public but in schools, where the minds of innocent children could be corrupted, was more unthinkable still.

And what role does David's father play in all this? Like many of the fathers in discussions of early pregnancy, he is largely invisible to the public eye. We do know that most fathers are relatively young themselves (about 80 percent of teenage mothers have a partner who is within five years of their own age). And we also have reason to suspect that this young man's faithful visits to the neonatal intensive care unit during David's lengthy stay there and his eager willingness to be a good father mark him as more typical than the stereotype would have it. Still, some twenty-five years after the most recent round of feminist activism, most people focus on teenage mothers instead of on young parents, so our knowledge about such men is surprisingly limited. . . .

Black and White

The public's apprehensions about poverty and dependency are in turn almost always intertwined with questions of race, given America's complex history on the matter. Many readers, in their mind's eye, will immediately see Michelle and her baby as African American, and this is understandable: the public quite commonly thinks of African Americans as prone to bear children at early ages and out of wedlock. The image is not false—but it's not entirely true, either. African Americans, who make up only about 15 percent of the population of teenage girls, account for more than a third of all teenage mothers. And whereas six out of every ten white teenagers who give birth are unmarried, among black teenagers the ratio is nine out of ten.

But although African Americans do account for a disproportionate share of births to teenagers and unmarried women, unmarried African American teenage mothers are not, statistically speaking, typical unwed teenage mothers. In 1990, for example, 57 percent of all babies born to unmarried teenage mothers were born to whites. And since 1985, birthrates among unmarried white teenagers have been increasing rapidly, while those among unmarried black teens have been largely stable. (Women of all ages—both African Americans and whites, married as well as unmarried—have been having more babies since 1988.)

Some commentators, among them Charles Murray, who has long been a critic of welfare policies and their putative effects on illegitimacy, say that the rising birthrates among white unmarried teenagers presage the growth of a white underclass, which will take its place alongside historically disadvantaged African Americans. In essence, Murray argues that as racial differences become less important in the life of the country, Americans will separate into two new nations—no longer black and white, but married and affluent on the one hand and unmarried and poor on the other.

Difficult Issues

So Michelle at her algebra exam and David at his bead game have come to represent a tangle of difficult issues—pertaining to sex, marriage, teenagers, race, dependency (as the condition of those who accept means-tested support from the government is conventionally labeled)—that confront the United States. . . . If we queried a stranger on the street and a neighbor over coffee, we would not be surprised to find that they, like much of the American public, find early pregnancy a very serious problem. Or that they have concluded that doing something about "babies having babies" is one way of confronting these troubling issues.

The Lowest Rate in Four Decades

[According to] officials of the National Center for Health Statistics, overall, births to teens ages 15 to 19 dropped in 1998 by 2 percent from 1997. They dropped 18 percent from 1991 through 1998.

Births to those in the 15-to-17 age group fell 5 percent in 1998—to 30.4 births for every 1,000 teens. That rate has dropped 21 percent since 1991—when it was 38.7 births—and is the lowest rate in at least four decades.

The birth rate among the youngest teens and preteens, ages 10 to 14, also fell 6 percent, to the lowest level since 1969. Still, 9,481 babies were born to young mothers in 1998.

African-American teen-agers recorded the lowest birth rate since 1960, when such data were first gathered, and the rate among Latinos also dropped precipitously, officials said.

Marc Lacey, *San Diego Union-Tribune*, October 27, 1999.

As with many issues that arouse a great deal of public worry and passion, that of "teenage pregnancy" is complex in nature and a challenge to conventional wisdom. Not only are Michelle and David more likely to be white than black, but as a high school student Michelle is younger than the statistically typical teenage mother. The majority of teenage mothers—almost six out of ten—are eighteen or nineteen when their babies are born, and they are legal adults in most states. Furthermore, although many people worry that pregnancy among teenagers has attained "epidemic" proportions, teenage women right now are having babies at about the same rate as they have for most of the twentieth century. The "epidemic" years were the 1950s, when teenagers were having twice as many babies as they had had in previous decades but few people worried about them. Even the teenage mothers who arouse the most concern—those who are under fifteen, the "babies having babies"—are simply doing what such "babies" did in the 1940s and 1950s, although they are more visible now than their counterparts were then.

Of course, it is true that in the 1950s almost all teenage mothers (in fact, almost all mothers) were married, at least by the time their babies arrived. But within the broader context—the number of babies being born to unmarried women—teenagers account for only a small subset of the problem. Two-thirds of unwed mothers are not teenagers, and in fact about one-fourth of America's unwed mothers are actually "no longer wed" mothers—that is, women who once were married but are not at the time their baby is born. . . .

Not Necessarily a Hardship

Despite what we all think we know about motherhood among teenagers and its effects on later life, having a baby as a teenager does not inevitably lead to abbreviated schooling and economic hardship, either for the mother or for the child. According to some older sources of data, pregnant teenagers *were* very likely to "truncate" their education, as the experts put it—but this curtailment resulted not so much from pregnancy per se as from the strictures that banned pregnant teachers and students from school grounds. Prior to 1975, when such policies were outlawed nationally, pregnant schoolgirls were "throwouts" more often than "dropouts." Now that secondary schools often have daycare facilities like the Sullivan Center, students who become pregnant in high school are increasingly likely to graduate and are beginning to do so at rates approaching those of nonpregnant teens. This is all the more surprising since the kinds of young people who get pregnant (and, in these days of legal abortion, *stay* pregnant) are usually the kinds of young people who are floundering in school long before a pregnancy occurs.

So if the easy assumptions about early pregnancy (that there's an epidemic of early births, that unwed mothers and teenage mothers are one and the same, that being a teenage mother is a short, quick route to poverty) aren't quite tenable, what do we know about pregnancy among teenagers? How did we come to think about it as a social problem? And what can we—should we—do about it?

In most of the public discussion of early pregnancy and motherhood that has taken place to date, the question about what we *should* do has predominated. Since pregnant teenagers in general and teenage mothers in particular raise such troubling questions about sex and gender, poverty and welfare, selfishness and altruism, self-indulgence and self-discipline, there is something approaching a consensus about what they and we should do. For their part, teenagers shouldn't have sex; if they have sex they should use contraception; if they get pregnant despite using contraception, they should have an abortion or give up the child for adoption; and failing all of that, they should marry the fathers of their babies. In terms of that amorphous "we" of the public, our obligation is to use moral suasion, economic incentives, and the whole repertoire of public policy to enable and sometimes coerce teenagers to do the right thing.

Deaf Ears

The only problem with such a consensus about what teenagers should do is that it seems to be falling on remarkably deaf ears. The picture here is a mixed one: teens are having more sex at the same time that they are using more contraception and using it more effectively. Compared with teenagers of twenty years ago, today's teens are getting pregnant less often but are also more likely, once pregnant, to go ahead and have their babies. Moreover, these days very few teens give up their children for adoption, and relatively few get married in order to make their babies "legal"—the two really notable revolutions in this area of American life.

On the national level it seems that society has re-created a situation familiar to all families with teenagers: adults are expressing strong, even violent opinions about what teenagers should be doing, and teenagers are just not listening. Not surprisingly, U.S. public policy concerning early pregnancy reflects the rather limited set of options that frustrated adults have at their disposal in the face of recalcitrant teenagers. Easygoing, liberal people conclude that the problem is merely lack of information: if adults just tell teenagers more clearly what they should do and why it's good for them, they will do it. More old-fashioned and authority-conscious people conclude that the problem is one of incentives and controls: if adults just cut off teens' allowance and limit their access to those privileges that society has under its control, teenagers will straighten up and do the right thing.

Neither of these strategies is working very well at present, and it is probably a waste of time to expend much more energy in this book or elsewhere debating whether "soft" or "tough" love is more effective in combating early pregnancy. The real question here is why teenagers do what they do, and how the world looks from their vantage point. Clearly, teenagers are not ignorant victims, but neither are they rational actors. The declining value of a welfare check over the last twenty years, and the increasingly tight eligibility requirements for receiving one in the first place, should make it immediately clear that if teenagers are simply "investors" they are exceedingly foolish ones.

Luckily, more than two decades of research on early pregnancy have given us a rich and complex body of information about teenagers and why they do what they do. The short answer to why teenagers get pregnant and especially to why they continue those pregnancies is that a fairly substantial number of them just don't believe what adults tell them, be it about sex, contraception, marriage, or babies. They don't believe in adult conventional wisdom—not because they are defiant or because they are developmentally too immature to process the information (although many are one or the other and some are both), but because the conventional wisdom does not accord with the world they see around them. When adults talk to teenagers, they draw on a lived reality that is now ten, twenty, thirty, forty or more years out of date. But today's teenagers live in a world whose demographic, social, economic, and sexual circumstances are almost unimaginable to older generations. Unless we can begin to understand that world, complete with its radically new circumstances, most of what adults tell teenagers will be just blather. . . .

America's Future

Michelle and David represent a challenge to American social attitudes and policies, one whose contours are only now becoming clear. As we consider the young woman at her algebra exam, her baby at play at the Sullivan Center, and the young man who cannot earn enough money to support that woman and child, we owe them our clearest thinking. In trying to find a way to better their lives and the lives of others like them, American society will have to confront some hard choices—choices that it would be easier to avoid facing. But to give these young people anything less than the nation's best effort would be a tragedy. For better or for worse, they are America's future.

"Men older than 20 . . . father five times more births among junior-high-school girls than do junior-high-school boys."

Teen Girls Are Sexually Exploited by Older Men

Oliver Starr Jr.

Studies have found that adult men are responsible for nearly three-fourths of all teen births, reports Oliver Starr Jr. in the following viewpoint. Moreover, the younger the girl, the greater the age difference is between her and her sexual partner, he maintains. Starr also asserts that older men often coerce their pregnant girlfriends into having abortions, are largely responsible for infecting their younger girlfriends with sexually transmitted diseases, and usually provide little or no financial support for their children. Starr concludes that society must make these predatory men responsible for their actions. Starr is a freelance writer.

As you read, consider the following questions:

1. What is the average age of the man who fathered a twelve-year-old girl's baby, according to Starr?
2. What evidence does the author present to support his contention that older men are responsible for spreading sexually transmitted diseases among young teen girls?
3. What percentage of teen mothers receive formal child support, according to the Congressional Budget Office as cited by the author?

The exploitation of teenage girls by older men may be one of the nation's most serious social problems, but it seldom is written or talked about. Approximately 900,000 teenage girls become pregnant each year; a little more than half of them give birth. The conventional wisdom is that their classmates father nearly all of these children. But a 1992 California Department of Health Services study showed that more than three-quarters of these children were fathered by men older than 20 and more than 70 percent of the births were out of wedlock. The study further found that men older than 20 also father five times more births among junior-high-school girls than do junior-high-school boys.

For girls in junior high, the father is on average 6.5 years older. When the mother is 12 years old or younger, the father averages 22. Most of these older fathers abandon their "used girls" like so many vessels of spoiled meat after getting them pregnant.

Manipulation, Coercion, and Abuse

"These studies highlight the problem that a substantial portion of teenage sexual activity is more a matter of manipulation, coercion or abuse than anything else," wrote Joe S. McIlhaney, gynecologist and expert on sexually transmitted diseases, in *Insight* (Sept. 29, 1997).

The 1996 "Kids Having Kids" study by the Robin Hood Foundation, a community-based relief agency in New York City, reached a similar conclusion. It says its research, conducted by leading scholars, "suggests that the incidence of pregnancy among adolescent girls often is a result of sexually predatory behavior of older men."

"Research also shows that about 25 percent of girls who become pregnant get that way under the influence of drugs and alcohol," says McIlhaney, founder of the Medical Institute for Sexual Health in Austin, Texas. "And we know how intense peer pressure is. It's a pit, a cesspool. Teens are not having 'beautiful, consensual sex' as is portrayed in films and TV. They are having horrible, manipulative sex that is saturated with drugs, alcohol and loneliness."

Studies of the causes of abortions show a continuing pattern of abuse. Steve Schwalm, former senior writer and analyst at the Family Research Council in Washington, recounts in the *Knight-Ridder/Tribune News* the case of a young pregnant woman and her boyfriend that occurred in August 1997 at the Hillcrest Women's Surgi-Center in Washington—not too far from the White House—where she planned to have an abortion.

Responding to the plea of a man outside the clinic "to love her baby and not go in," she abruptly changed her mind and sat down on a red brick wall as her boyfriend continued inside. In seconds, he returned and badgered her for about a half-hour, trying to make her go in for the abortion. She refused.

The boyfriend "then hit the woman on the face and she tumbled to the ground. He continued beating her in the face and then sat on her and beat her some more, according to police, until clinic workers lifted her up and took her into the abortion center," Schwalm reported.

One would have expected an outcry not just in Washington but nationally about this pregnant woman being so savagely beaten by the baby's father, trying to force her to have an abortion. But there was no outcry, "not even a mention of this incident by groups ostensibly founded to defend women's rights," says Schwalm.

It turns out that this kind of abusive behavior by boyfriends toward women and girls they have impregnated is common and goes largely unreported by the media. The following data cited by Schwalm shows a pattern of coercion in abortions, refuting the common view that they almost always are consensual:

• The Elliot Institute reports that about 40 percent of abortion cases involve coercion.

• A survey of members of the organization Women Exploited by Abortion showed 33 percent were encouraged to have abortions by their boyfriends—higher than even the percentage (27 percent) pushed in that direction by abortion counselors.

• Fifty-four percent of the respondents also said they felt "forced by outside circumstances" to have an abortion.

• Husbands pushed for abortion the least, at only 9 percent.

Sexually Transmitted Diseases

The media also seldom mention the venereal-disease epidemic plaguing the nation and hitting teenagers particularly hard. Three million teenage girls and boys—approximately 20 percent of teens who are sexually active—become infected with a sexually transmitted disease every year.

How disproportionate this is to the adult population can be seen in the fact that teenagers account for 25 percent of all cases of sexually transmitted diseases even though they make up only about 10 percent of the population. AIDS commonly is thought to seldom strike the young, but the National Institutes of Allergy and Infectious Disease in 1996 found that 25 percent of all new HIV infections in the United States are estimated to occur in young people between ages 13 and 20.

Men and Girls

According to the Arizona Department of Health Services, 66.3 percent of the babies born to teenage girls in 1994 were fathered by men age 20 or older.

The Washington Alliance Concerned with School Age Parents conducted a survey in Seattle of mothers ages 12 to 17 in 1995 and found the average age of the fathers was 24.

An article in the *American Journal of Public Health* in 1996 cited statistics for California's teen mothers. In 1993, wrote authors Mike Males and Kenneth S.Y. Chew, two-thirds of school-age teen mothers had a post-school-age partner.

Arizona Republic, July 9, 1996.

So little has been reported about the VD epidemic that the Institute of Medicine titled its 1997 report on the outbreak *The Hidden Epidemic—Confronting Sexually Transmitted Disease*. Federal and local public-health officials say "the United States is in the throes of an epidemic of sexually transmitted diseases that in poor, underserved areas such as Baltimore's inner city rivals that of some developing nations," Sheryl Gay Stolberg reported in the *New York Times* in March 1999.

King K. Holmes, professor of medicine at the University of Washington, says that a "conspiracy of silence" has allowed sexually transmitted infections to flourish. The number of new sexual-disease cases each year has increased from 10 million to 12 million. These include high rates of human papilloma virus, chlamydia and herpes—as well as serious local outbreaks of syphilis and gonorrhea.

"A study released last October [1997] found that one in five Americans older than 12 was infected with the genital herpes virus, a 30 percent increase from two decades ago. Rates among white teenagers quadrupled," she said.

The evidence points once more to men older than 20 as major spreaders of venereal disease among teenage girls. The Centers for Disease Control and Prevention in 1996 warned: "These adult/youth sex patterns have profound implications for the spread of sexually transmitted disease, or STD, and AIDS as well. STD and AIDS rates are 2.5 times higher among females under age 20 than can be predicted from rates among males under age 20. . . . This points strongly to STD transmission from older men."

Fathers Provide Little Support

Most of the older-than-20 men and high-school boys who father these out-of-wedlock children also refuse to provide any kind of support, financial or otherwise, for the teenage girls they impregnate or their children. "More than half of teenage mothers are not residing with their child's father by the time the child reaches grade school. More than one-quarter have never lived with the father," Suzanne Chazin reported in *Reader's Digest*. "Nor does the father offer much (financial) help: only 20 percent of never-married mothers receive formal child support, according to the Congressional Budget Office."

The social and economic costs of these teenage-pregnancy, abortion and STD epidemics are enormous. They have been estimated to run as high as $21 billion a year. Taking care of a baby without the help of the father is a full-time job, often preventing the teenage mother from earning money she needs to support herself and the child, which is why eight out of 10 of these girls go on welfare, where a great many of them and their children often remain for a generation or more.

Dependent families formed by teenage mothers consume

more than half of all welfare money spent. Nearly 30 percent of unmarried mothers stay poor during their twenties and thirties, the critically important developmental years of their children. Only three of 10 girls who become pregnant at the age of 17 or younger will earn a high-school diploma by age 30, as contrasted with 76 percent of women who delay child-bearing until the age of 20 or older, according to the "Kids Having Kids" study.

The Younger the Girl, the Older the Man

Two recent studies shed new light on the subject of teen pregnancy. A survey by the National Center for Health Statistics notes that 67 percent of teenage mothers are im-pregnated by men who are over 20 years old. In other words, approximately 700,000 teenage pregnancies every year in-volve men who are 20 to 50 years old. Whether coerced or voluntary, couplings between teenage girls and adult males are many times more likely to result in pregnancy than teen-teen sex. In fact, the younger the girl, the older the man. Several other studies are equally shocking: researchers Debra Boyer and David Fine note that two-thirds of young women who become pregnant during adolescence have previously been sexually abused or raped, nearly always by fathers, step-fathers, other relatives or guardians.

Linda Villarosa, *Third Force*, March/April 1996.

Children of unmarried teenage girls also have much more severe problems than children of married parents. The same study points out:

• Teenage sons of adolescent mothers are 2.7 times more likely to go to prison than the sons of mothers who delay childbearing until their early twenties.

• Children of teenage mothers have more trouble in school. They perform significantly worse on tests.

• Performance in school does not improve as children of adolescent mothers age; they are far more likely to drop out than are children born to later childbearers.

Deadbeat Dads

It is ironic that a society that vigorously prosecutes hit-and-run drivers does so little to stop the impregnate-and-run men who cumulatively have ruined the lives of many millions of teenage girls by making them pregnant and then taking off for parts unknown.

Despite their unsavory, predatory record, the disappearing deadbeat dads of out-of-wedlock children seem to find another bumper crop of teenage girls each year willing to rush into their arms for a trip down nightmare alley and poverty row. Isn't it time to track down these delinquent deadbeat dads and make them pay for what they've done? Somehow, teenage girls have got to get the message that going out with these older men is like the proverbial fly's acceptance to visit the spider's web.

| *"Most of the first sexual partners of teenage*
| *girls are teenage boys."*

Most Teens' Sex Partners Are Close in Age

Kristin A. Moore and Anne Driscoll

A national study of more than 10,000 women and girls found that most teen girls are close in age to their sexual partners, report Kristin A. Moore and Anne Driscoll in the following viewpoint. The study also discovered that the closer the ages are between a teen girl and her first sexual partner, the more likely they are to use contraception, the fewer partners the girl will have during her teen years, and the less likely she will be to give birth while a teen. Furthermore, Moore and Driscoll assert, girls who grow up with both biological parents in the home are less likely to have sex than teen girls who grow up without fathers or with stepfathers. Moore is president of Child Trends, Inc., a research organization that studies children, adolescents, and families. Driscoll is a fellow with Child Trends.

As you read, consider the following questions:

1. What percentage of girls were "going steady" with their first sexual partner, according to Moore and Driscoll?
2. What reason do the authors give for why contraception use declines as the difference in age increases between teen girls and their sexual partners?
3. Why are teen girls who live with both parents less likely to have sex as teenagers, according to the authors?

It goes without saying that males are involved in teen pregnancy. However, most research has focused on teenage girls, as has most policy and media attention. The National Campaign to Prevent Teen Pregnancy, with the Washington, DC-based research organization Child Trends, Inc., presents here analyses from the most current nationally representative data on sex, pregnancy, and childbearing available to inform the discussion on teen pregnancy and its prevention. The following information is based on analyses of the 1995 National Survey of Family Growth (NSFG), a periodic survey conducted by the National Center for Health Statistics of the Department of Health and Human Services that collects data on the factors affecting pregnancy, health, and childbearing of women in the United States. The sample interviewed consists of 10,847 women aged 15 to 44. The information below is drawn from a subsample of the NSFG consisting of young women aged 15 to 19. . . .

Although the National Survey of Family Growth is a survey of females, important information is available on the men in their lives. This allows for some analyses of the role of males in teenage pregnancy and its prevention. In order to capture the multiple roles of men, we present information from three different perspectives. First, we look at males as the sexual partners of teen girls; specifically, we present information about teens' first sexual partners. Second, we present information on the phenomenon of non-voluntary and unwanted first sexual experiences in which teen girls were either victims of coercion or ambivalent about the timing or other aspects of their first sexual experience. Third, we look at the role that fathers may play in protecting their daughters from early sexual initiation and its consequences.

Adolescent Girls and Their First Sex Partners

Data on male partners are available for girls who described their first sex as voluntary. In most cases, teen girls know their first sexual partners fairly well. For 73 percent of them, their first sexual partner is someone they have been "going steady" with; another 20 percent were friends with their first partner or dated him occasionally.

Most teenage girls are relatively close in age to their first sexual partner at first intercourse; in other words, they are peers. While 12 percent of teen girls had a first partner who was five or more years older, 18 percent had partners the same age or younger, 43 percent had partners a year or two older, and the rest (27 percent) had partners three to four years older. This pattern suggests that most of the first sexual partners of teenage girls are teenage boys.

Important Correlations

Although often not great, the difference in age between a teenage girl and her first sexual partner appears to be correlated with several important factors. This is particularly significant for girls with much older partners for whom a large age difference may signal similarly large differences in the power balance of the relationship and of the communication and negotiation within it. One of these factors is the likelihood of using contraception. The closer in age teen girls and their partners are, the more likely they are to have reported using contraception at first sex. Significant increases in condom use by teens have occurred over the past decade; three-quarters of teen girls whose first partner was within a year of their own age used birth control compared to only two-thirds of teens whose first partner was five or more years older. Moreover, the decline in contraception as age differences increase is due to declines in condom use, suggesting that older partners may be less willing and/or feel less compunction to use condoms with much younger partners. The consequences of this situation can be serious. Teens with older partners are less likely to be protected against not only pregnancy, but also sexually transmitted diseases (STDs), including AIDS.

The age difference between teen girls and their first partners is related to their own age at first sex. The younger a girl is when she has sex for the first time, the greater the average age difference between her and her partner. For example, only 18 percent of girls who were younger than 14 when they first had sex had a partner who was within a year of their age; this was the case for 37 percent of teens who were 14–15 years old at first sex, and for more than half of teens who were 16 years old or older. Given the pattern between age differences and contraception at first sex, teen girls who have sex at very young ages appear to be particularly at risk for having unprotected sex.

Most Girls Are Close in Age to Their First Sexual Partner

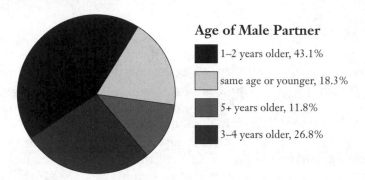

Age of Male Partner

◼ 1–2 years older, 43.1%

▢ same age or younger, 18.3%

▨ 5+ years older, 11.8%

◼ 3–4 years older, 26.8%

Kristin A. Moore and Anne Driscoll, *Not Just for Girls: The Roles of Boys and Men in Teen Pregnancy Prevention*, 1997.

The narrower the age difference between teen girls and their first partners, the fewer the number of sexual partners they go on to have during their teen years. While only one-third of teen girls whose first partner was two years older or more have no additional partners as teens, 42 percent of those girls whose partners were closer in age to themselves have no other partners. Conversely, 36 percent of teen girls with similar-age partners have two or more additional partners as teens, while 56 percent of teen girls whose first partners were five or more years older have two or more additional partners. Multiple partners is associated with a higher risk of contracting an STD. Given that the analyses reported here are preliminary, the reasons for the pattern of greater age differences and number of sexual partners are not yet clear. However, it is likely that wider age differences are related to earlier age at first sex; the younger teen girls are when they first have sex, the longer they are at risk during their teen years of having additional partners.

The size of the age difference between teen girls and their first partners is also correlated with the likelihood of ever giving birth while a teen. Teens whose first partner was five or more years older are almost twice as likely to have a birth during their teen years as teens whose first partner was within a year of their own age (24 percent vs. 13 percent).

Males as Predators

The public and policymakers have often assumed that teens' decisions to have sex are, at worst, ill-thought-out and spontaneous ("it just sort of happened") or, at best, the result of rational decision-making on the part of teen girls, after weighing what they perceive as the costs and benefits of the situation. Recently, recognition that many adolescents experience coercive sex has led to a focus on non-voluntary sex. Due to the inclusion of questions in the 1995 NSFG on the voluntary nature and degree of wantedness of first sex, we now have up-to-date information on the extent to which first sex is not under the control of young women.

Of teen girls aged 15 to 19 who have had sex, 7 percent reported that their first experience was not voluntary (including girls who said they were raped). Another 24 percent said that while the experience was voluntary on their part, they did not want to have sex when they did. The rest, 69 percent, said that their first sexual experience was both voluntary and wanted. These statistics raise important issues to be considered in designing teen pregnancy prevention efforts. First, attention must be paid to the risk factors of non-voluntary sex and to helping teen girls avoid this experience. Second, prevention initiatives must take into account that more than two-thirds of girls who first have sex as teens do so voluntarily.

Non-voluntary first sex is particularly common among very young girls. Among girls who had sex before they were 13 years old, 22 percent reported that first sex was non-voluntary, and an additional 49 percent categorized it as unwanted. These figures decline among those whose first sex occurred when they were 13 or 14 years old: 8 percent reported that their first sex was non-voluntary, and another 31 percent had unwanted first sex. Among those who first had sex when they were 15 or 16, for 5 percent it was non-voluntary, and for 19 percent it was unwanted. These numbers highlight the

Percentage Distribution of Pregnancies, Births and Abortions to Women Aged 15–17, by Age of Partner

Age of partner	Women (N= 1,517,000)	Pregnancies (N= 447,100)	Intended births (N=93,900)	Unintended births (N=214,200)	Abortions (N= 139,100)
2 yrs. older/ younger	64.1	50.0	44.1	43.4	64.1
3–5 yrs. older	29.2	30.8	28.1	34.4	27.1
6 yrs. older	6.7	19.2	27.9	22.2	8.8
Total	100.0	100.0	100.0	100.0	100.0

Note: Numbers may not sum to total due to rounding.

Jacqueline E. Darroch, David J. Landry, and Selene Oslak, *Family Planning Perspectives*, July/August 1999.

need to protect young girls against sexual predation.

Teen girls who classified their first sexual experience as voluntary but unwanted were more likely to be considerably younger than their partners. One-quarter of girls whose partners were the same age or younger described their first sex as unwanted. This rises to 37 percent of teen girls whose first partners were five or more years older, indicating that a discrepancy in age seems to be related to a power imbalance within the relationship.

The Presence of Fathers

Teen girls who grew up with both their biological parents during their entire time at home are less likely to have sex than are teens who grew up under any other family structure. While 43 percent of teen girls with both parents have ever had sex by their twentieth birthday, 60 percent of all other teen girls have. The reasons for this association are not clear. Growing up with both parents may allow for more monitoring by parents of where their teen daughters are and who they are with. It may block the possibility of other grown males, like stepfathers or mothers' boyfriends, from living in the household and having access to those teens. The generally higher income of married men may provide safer neighborhoods for their daughters and furnish the means for them to participate in activities that remove them from circumstances under which sex is likely to take place. Being raised by an intact parental couple may serve as a model for sexual relationships within marriage; similarly, growing up in such an environment may allow girls to learn more positive relationship skills for interacting with men. These and other hypotheses remain to be tested, however.

Teen girls with both biological parents are less likely to have sex, including non-voluntary first sex, than other teen girls. However, they are no more likely to use contraception the first time they have sex than teen girls from other family backgrounds. Teen girls raised by both parents are less likely to become teen mothers, probably at least in part due to their lower likelihood of having sex at all.

Simplistic Discussions

Discussions of the causes of adolescent pregnancy tend to be simplistic; similarly, interventions tend to be simplistic, seeking a single, "magic bullet" solution. Too much of the discussion about the role of males in teen pregnancy has focused on the concept of men as predators. Males can play several different roles, however—as the peer-age partners of teen girls, as the older partners who may force teen girls to have sex, and as fathers who protect their daughters from teenage sex and its consequences. The National Survey of Adolescent Males sheds more light on the role that males play as peers. The picture drawn here, preliminary as it is, offers a basis for further research and discussion around several important points:

- Most teen girls who have sex have a prior relationship with their first partners, are fairly close in age to them, used contraception at first sex, and report that their first sexual experience was not only voluntary but wanted.
- However, significant minorities of teen girls experienced non-voluntary or unwanted first sex, especially those who were younger when they first had sex.
- In addition, a sizable minority of teen girls reported not

using any form of contraception at first sex. Among teen girls who had voluntary sex, those whose first partners were considerably older than they were somewhat less likely to use any form of contraception.

- Girls raised throughout childhood by both of their biological parents are less likely to have sex as teenagers and are less likely to become teen parents.

Better appreciation and knowledge of these and related issues should be used to create effective teen pregnancy prevention programs that protect teen girls from coerced sex and that involve boys and men in positive ways.

Periodical Bibliography

The following articles have been selected to supplement the diverse views presented in this chapter. Addresses are provided for periodicals not indexed in the *Readers' Guide to Periodical Literature*, the *Alternative Press Index*, the *Social Sciences Index*, or the *Index to Legal Periodicals and Books*.

B. Drummond Ayres Jr. "Marriage Advised in Some Youth Pregnancies," *New York Times*, September 9, 1996.

Suzanne Chazin "Teen Pregnancy: Let's Get Real," *Reader's Digest*, September 1996.

Jacqueline E. Darroch, David J. Landry, and Selene Oslak "Age Differences Between Sexual Partners in the United States," *Family Planning Perspectives*, July/August 1999.

Arline T. Geronimus "Teenage Childbearing and Personal Responsibility: An Alternative View," *Political Science Quarterly*, Fall 1997.

Tamar Lewin "Birth Rates for Teen-Agers Declined Sharply in the 90s," *New York Times*, May 1, 1998.

Jeffrey S. Luke and Kathryn Robb Neville "Curbing Teen Pregnancy: A Divided Community Acts Together," *Responsive Community*, Summer 1998.

Jeannie I. Rosoff "Helping Teenagers Avoid Negative Consequences of Sexual Activity," *USA Today*, May 1996.

Kathleen Sylvester "Preventable Calamity: How to Reduce Teenage Pregnancy," *USA Today*, March 1997.

Emory Thomas Jr. "Is Pregnancy a Rational Choice for Poor Teenagers?" *Wall Street Journal*, January 18, 1996.

Linda Villarosa "Who's Really Makin' Babies?" *Third Force*, March/April 1996.

CHAPTER 3

How Should Society Respond to Teen Sex?

Chapter Preface

Since the *Roe* v. *Wade* decision in 1973, which legalized abortions under the Constitution's right to privacy, the U.S. Supreme Court has gradually extended the right to privacy to teenagers as well. Teens can receive confidential reproductive health services, such as contraceptives, pregnancy tests and counseling, abortions, screenings and treatment for sexually transmitted diseases (STDs), all without their parents' knowledge or consent.

Many parents are against such confidential health services. They believe that teen access to confidential treatment infringes on parents' rights to raise their children and to control their medical care without outside interference. Access to confidential health services undermines parental authority and the stability of the family, they contend, which is not in teens' best interests. Furthermore, opponents argue that many teenagers are not mature enough to make responsible decisions about their sexuality. Janna C. Merrick, an expert in health care policy at the University of South Florida, asserts, "I find it absolutely ludicrous to argue that a 14-year-old is mature enough to obtain confidential medical services related to her sexuality, but too immature to drive a car, purchase alcohol, or vote."

However, advocates of confidential health services argue that confidentiality is in teens' best interests. They contend that if parents are informed about requests for contraceptives, the result will not be fewer teens having sex but fewer teens requesting contraceptives. A study of sexually active teens found that half would not use contraceptives if their parents had to be notified, while less than 2 percent said they would stop having sex. Consequently, asserts the Planned Parenthood Affiliates of California, sexually active teens "will be more likely to become pregnant, to contract sexually transmitted disease, and to seek abortions," results that are definitely not in the teens' best interests.

The authors in the following chapter examine the struggle over the rights of the individual versus the rights of society and the family in issues that concern public health and morality.

> *"There are millions of responsible teens out there . . . who are living proof that younger Americans are quite capable of waiting at least until they are adults before becoming sexually active."*

Society Should Encourage Teens to Postpone Sex Until Marriage

Joseph Perkins

In the following viewpoint, Joseph Perkins contends that teenagers can and should be taught to postpone sexual activity until marriage. In fact, he maintains, more and more teens are practicing abstinence thanks to a new federal grant program that requires states to teach the benefits of abstinence in schools. Furthermore, Perkins asserts, since schools have begun teaching abstinence-only sex education in schools, the rates for teenage pregnancy, abortion, and birth have fallen. Teens will be less inclined to become sexually active before marriage if they are taught that abstinence until marriage is normal and expected behavior, he argues. Perkins is an editorial writer for the *San Diego Union-Tribune*.

As you read, consider the following questions:
1. Why is Alexandra Stevenson notable, in the author's opinion?
2. What provided a major boost to the abstinence-only movement, according to Perkins?
3. What was the average age in 1998 of a teen's first sexual experience, as cited by Perkins?

Reprinted, with permission, from Joseph Perkins, "The Best Choice for Teens Concerning Sex," *San Diego Union-Tribune*, August 13, 1997.

Alexandra Stevenson, a recent graduate of La Jolla [California] Country Day School, raised a lot of eyebrows when she made it all the way to the Wimbledon semifinals. And the 18-year-old almost certainly raised as many eyebrows when she revealed in a nationally televised interview that she has never been kissed.

Indeed, it's one thing for a teen-ager to make an overnight transition from a promising high school tennis player to a serious contender for a Grand Slam tennis title. But to think that she made it all the way through high school without having sex, without having so much as a kiss. Forget about it.

Not Such an Aberration

Well, as it happens, young Alexandra is not such an aberration. In fact, an increasing number of her fellow teens are also practicing chastity. And much of the credit for this must go the growing number of abstinence-only programs that are reaching youngsters throughout the country.

The teen-abstinence movement got a major boost by the 1996 welfare reform law, which included a provision setting aside $250 million over five years for a federal program to discourage teen sex.

The ground rules of the program are to teach younger Americans "the social, psychological and health gains to be realized by abstaining from sexual activity" and to caution teens that "sexual activity outside of . . . marriage is likely to have harmful psychological and physical effects."

States can get a share of the federal money by putting up $3 for every $4 they request from Washington. The maximum yearly grant a state may receive is $5.7 million, which the state must match with $4.2 million of its own.

Since 1997, the states have created nearly 700 new abstinence-only programs, bringing the nationwide total to roughly 1,000. And even the lone state government that has chosen not to participate in the federal program, California, is funding abstinence-only programs out of state coffers.

This represents a radical shift in public policy with respect to teens and sex. For the past quarter-century, at least, the prevailing wisdom has been that the government ought not waste time and tax dollars trying to discourage the under-aged from having sex.

The more "realistic" and "sensible" approach, the thinking went, was for the government to bend its efforts to preventing unwanted pregnancies and sexually transmitted diseases by supporting programs that make condoms and birth control pills more readily available to youngsters.

Sex Is Power

The operative thesis, which has been proved for several thousand years now, is that women control the sexual territory.

The message to girls should be: Sex Is Power. Save it, horde it, use it wisely, give it seldom. . . .

The truth is: *Not* having sex is power. The reason? Because girls get pregnant; boys don't. Boys don't pray over the toilet bowl; they walk. Girls have abortions; boys don't. . . .

Our message needs to be: Girls, sex is power. Don't give it away.

Kathleen Parker, *San Diego Union-Tribune*, July 21, 1997.

Well, this "teens-will-be-teens" orthodoxy has not withered away by any stretch of the imagination, but it does face a serious challenge today from the abstinence-only movement. And this challenge has the "sex education" crowd (which teaches chastity as one of several sexual "options" for kids) plenty worried.

And with good cause. The abstinence-only movement is producing desired results. Indeed, since federal funds started flowing to abstinence-only programs in 1997, the number of teen-age pregnancies, abortions and births have fallen. Moreover, the average age at which youngsters have their first sexual experience has risen from 15.8 in 1997 to 16.3 in 1998, according to the Durex Global Survey.

The Prevailing Wisdom About Teen Sex

These developments show that the prevailing wisdom about teen sex—that kids simply cannot control their raging hormones, that they are bound to have sex—is a fallacy. Kids live up or down to expectations.

Indeed, if adults impart the message to teens that they are

expected to be sexually active, that it's OK as long as they use a condom or take the pill, then those teens are that much more likely to engage in sexual activity.

On the other hand, if teens get the message that under-age, premarital sex is not normative, that adults will not tacitly condone teen promiscuity by providing contraceptives-on-demand, no questions asked, then youngsters will be less inclined to have sex.

There are millions of responsible teens out there, like Alexandra Stevenson, who are living proof that younger Americans are quite capable of waiting at least until they are adults before becoming sexually active.

They recognize that the best way to avoid unwanted pregnancies and sexually transmitted diseases is not by practicing so-called "safe sex"—by using condoms and birth control pills—but by refraining from sex altogether.

> *"I consider it to have been a real plus that I did not enter my now 13-year 'faithful monogamous relationship in the context of marriage' as a virgin."*

Premarital Teen Sex Is Normal

Eric Zorn

Surveys have found that most men and women are not virgins when they marry, reports Eric Zorn in the following viewpoint. According to Zorn, sex education programs that teach only abstinence to teenagers are ineffective at convincing teens to delay sex until marriage. Although he maintains that trying to persuade teens to postpone sex until marriage—or at least until the later teen years—is a worthy goal, premarital teen sex is standard, normal behavior. Zorn is a syndicated columnist.

As you read, consider the following questions:
1. What percent of men and women in the *Bride's* magazine reported they were virgins when they married, according to the author?
2. How many sex partners did the women in the *Bride's* survey report having, other than their husbands-to-be, as cited by Zorn?
3. What are the key elements of sexual responsibility, according to Zorn?

Reprinted from "Save It for Marriage? Most of Us Rewrote That Fact of Life," by Eric Zorn, *Liberal Opinion*, July 20, 1998. Reprinted with permission from Knight Ridder/Tribune Information Services.

Readers of *Bride's* may be an unusually randy bunch, so we must use some caution in approaching the results of the magazine's wedding-night survey published in its August/September 1998 issue.

Out of 3,000 engaged couples who responded, just 4 percent of the women and 1 percent of the men reported that they will be virgins when they exchange vows. For women, the figure was down from 14 percent in a similar *Bride's* survey in 1988, and on average, the women in 1998 reported having had six other sex partners aside from their husbands-to-be.

More scientific surveys have put the wedding-virginity rate at 7 to 16 percent for men and 20 to 30 percent for women, but either way the numbers suggest two things:

1. The federal guidelines for abstinence-only education—a fad pushed by social and religious conservatives and funded generously by taxpayers—are based on wishful thinking.

2. The "But what did you do, mom and dad?" question about sex is going to be even more awkward for today's parents than the same question has been about illegal-drug usage.

The guidelines for state programs taking advantage of the $50 million Congress now allocates annually for no-sex education say teachers must tell students that "abstinence from sexual activity outside marriage (is) the expected standard . . . (and) that a mutually faithful monogamous relationship in the context of marriage is the expected standard of human sexual activity."

Premarital Sex Is Standard Behavior

In reality, however, pre-marital and non-marital sex are standard practice in this country. An expectation that the man and woman you see standing at an altar or in front of a justice of the peace have never had sex is likely to be crushed by the truth.

Abstinence-only backers respond that "standard" here refers to a moral requirement, not a mathematical result or popularity poll. Pre-marital sex is bad, they say. Or, in the language of the federal guidelines: "Sexual activity outside the context of marriage is likely to have harmful psychological and physical effects."

But what did you do, mom and dad? Survey says . . . you probably indulged in the deed without the benefit of clergy at least a time or two. And it's my guess you weren't just "experimenting," the No. 1 old drug-use dodge, and you'd be less than candid if you said that you consider it all "a mistake," the No. 2 dodge.

Sometimes it was a mistake, of course. Sexuality is a complicated thing—dynamite in all metaphorical senses. When it explodes in your face, it's often because you misunderstood it, yourself or someone else.

Reprinted by permission of Chip Bok and the Creator's Syndicate.

When it doesn't explode, it can take you to new levels of intimacy where you learn valuable lessons about yourself and gain some of the perspective necessary for wisdom. This comes in handy later when you're pondering lifelong commitments.

Through such relationships you can learn what sex is and what it isn't; who you are and who you are not. Speaking for myself—one who belongs in the mainstream of *Bride's* readership, so to speak—I have regrets about certain indiscretions and related pain both received and inflicted. But overall I consider it to have been a real plus that I did not enter my now 13-year "faithful monogamous relationship in the context of marriage" as a virgin.

What to Tell the Kids

What to tell the kids? They can smell hypocrisy at 100 yards, and "just say no" coming from an experienced generation that just said "oh, yes" is not likely to be persuasive, even in an age when sexually transmitted diseases pose a greater threat than in the past.

Yet that very experience also tells what we can say without reservation: Delay, restraint, moderation, contraception, love and respect are key elements of sexual responsibility. Holding off until at least the late teen years is by far the wisest choice.

Abstinence is a fine idea. It was never presented as an option to students in my schools in the 1970s, and it should have been.

But "abstinence-only" is an opinion. And, as today's brides and grooms tell us, a minority opinion at that.

*"The common-law provision . . . is to
pronounce any sexual intercourse with
underage girls as . . . rape."*

Society Should Enforce Laws Against Teen Sex

William F. Buckley Jr.

In the mid-1990s, several pregnant teen girls and their
boyfriends in Idaho were arrested and convicted of fornication—a little-known and rarely enforced law that prohibits
unmarried people from having sex—and statutory rape, which
prohibits sex with minors under a specified age. In the following viewpoint, William F. Buckley Jr. maintains that society is
right to enforce such laws against unwed teen mothers and fathers because their babies exact high costs on society; their
children are more likely to be poorly educated, take drugs, go
to prison, or be on welfare, he asserts. Enforcing these laws
against teens who engage in sex may prevent other teen pregnancies, Buckley contends. Buckley is president and editor of
the *National Review* and a syndicated columnist.

As you read, consider the following questions:

1. What teens were the target of Idaho's laws against
   fornication and statutory rape, according to Buckley?
2. What is the maximum sentence for "lewd and lascivious
   behavior," as cited by the author?
3. What is the paradox that develops in a free society, in
   Buckley's opinion?

Reprinted from "Enforce the Law in Idaho," by William F. Buckley Jr., *The
Washington Times*, July 12, 1996. Reprinted with permission from Universal Press
Syndicate.

The *Wall Street Journal* reports Gem County, Idaho, is conducting a daredevil experiment with the law—by enforcing it. Sitting in the statute books all these years is a little derelict that says that "any unmarried person who shall have sex with an unmarried person of the opposite sex shall be found guilty of fornication."

Pregnant Teens Are the Target

The county prosecutor whose bright idea was to apply the law didn't do so indiscriminately. To have done this would of course have meant to repeal the Playboy Philosophy, and nobody thinks himself grand or powerful enough to accomplish that. But Douglas Varie decided to focus on just one fruit of the law: teen-age pregnancy.

As everybody (almost everybody) knows, there is such a thing as prosecutorial discretion, which means that you can't defy the cop who stops you for speeding on the grounds that he didn't stop the other guy for speeding. There are exceptions. If prosecutorial conduct bumps into civil rights laws, then intervention by the courts can be tried. If only Hispanics or women are stopped for speeding, they can complain and get a hospitable hearing.

But Mr. Varie didn't start snooping around in motels or parking lots overlooking the scenic splendors of the state of Idaho. He started looking for pregnant teen-agers. In fact, he narrowed the search still further. He has been looking for pregnant teen-agers who apply for federal and state welfare.

Having done this, he then looks for the feller who got her in the family way. And although this is often another teenager, sometimes it is not, for instance in a recent case in which Michael Hopkins, the stud in question, was 22 years old. The penalty for lewd and lascivious behavior can be life imprisonment. Nobody expects this to happen, but the mere thought of it might interfere with Michael's self-confidence in future encounters.

One pregnant girl was sentenced to 30 days for a misdemeanor and she was quite shocked by the severity of the sentence. The prosecutor pointed out that the community had every right to be shocked at the prospect of a child being born out of wedlock, which increases by a very high percentage the probability that that child will end up in prison, on welfare, illiterate and on drugs.

Thorough and Systematic Enforcement

In the case of teen-age pregnancies, all that is needed is thorough and systematic enforcement of laws pertaining to statutory rape. A girl of 16 and under has, by law, been raped, whether she consented to or even initiated the sex act. She should be required to name and testify against the male, of any age, who should be prosecuted for rape and given the maximum penalty. . . .

If these predatory males knew for certain that they would face prison and fines for every casual roll in the hay, you would see a tremendous decline in the teen-age pregnancies that result. In addition to fines and imprisonment, these men can be compelled to support their illegitimate offspring, which would free government from becoming surrogate parents.

Ralph de Toledano, *Conservative Chronicle*, August 28, 1996.

Needless to say, the American Civil Liberties Union has got into the act, though it isn't absolutely clear what case it has. The prosecutor asked the general question: Does the community intend to enforce the law against statutory rape? This is defined as a sexual encounter with a girl under a certain age. What does one do, he asked, in a situation in which a 15-year-old girl is made pregnant, say by a 22-year-old man, and declines to charge her companion with rape? The common-law provision in such cases is to pronounce any sexual intercourse with underage girls as that exactly—rape. And whatever ambiguities beset the law when deciding whether sexual congress took place, there aren't any when the girl is pregnant.

The Free Society Paradox

The Idaho experiment reminds us once again of a paradox in the development of social practices in free societies. It is that these societies suffer from heavy criticism of their toughness (the Darwinian reproach) but shrink from getting the benefits from toughness. We terribly much want American children to learn to read and write, and we offer them public facilities in which to learn how to do this. But if they refuse to learn, we do—nothing. We very much desire that youngsters do not band together in gangs that harass innocent people, but on the whole, we do nothing about them. We terribly want boys and girls not to create children doomed to neglect, but far from discouraging such activity, we subsidize it.

A free society is one that in most cases imposes penalties by its own devices. If you start a mousetrap factory and produce a product less successful than that of your competitors, what happens is that you go broke. The people who work for you lose their jobs, you lose your capital, and the empty factory building is auctioned off. But if you create one of the 1 million children born out of wedlock every year, you pass along the welfare cost to the government and, as often as not, produce another child.

Mr. Varie in Idaho thinks that is not a good idea and has come up with the ingenious solution of activating, in however diluted form, the law. Very much worth watching, Gem County, Idaho.

*"Punishment is the political path of least
resistance when it comes to thorny social
issues such as discouraging teens from
having babies. Certainly, such prosecutions
do nothing to encourage pregnant teens to
seek help."*

Laws Against Teen Sex Are Ineffective

Robin Abcarian

Prosecuting teens who become pregnant is an ineffective way
of discouraging teen pregnancy, contends Robin Abcarian in
the following viewpoint. In fact, she asserts, criminalizing teen
sex is more likely to result in the concealment of pregnancies,
thus denying teenage girls the help and care they need. In addition, Abcarian argues, prosecuting teen sex may convince
teens that abortion is the best solution to an unwanted pregnancy. Abcarian is a columnist for the *Los Angeles Times*.

As you read, consider the following questions:

1. What was Amanda Smisek's sentence for fornication, as
   cited by Abcarian?
2. What percentage of the babies born to California's teen
   mothers were fathered by men twenty and older,
   according to the California Senate Office of Research?
3. How did the prosecutions of Amanda Smisek and Kirsten
   Sundberg differ, according to the author?

I n the waning days of the 20th century, there are many ways a gal can end up on the wrong side of the law, but this one came as a surprise even to me: Amanda Smisek, a high school senior with good grades, was convicted in 1996 of fornication.

Yes, you read that right.

Amanda lives in Emmett, Idaho. And in Idaho, unfortunately, there remains on the books an anti-fornication statute that makes it a crime for two unmarried people to have sex.

Worthy Goal, Loony Method

One Idaho prosecutor has revived this once-forgotten law with a vengeance and has brought charges against at least eight girls and their boyfriends. The idea, apparently, is to discourage teen pregnancy, a perfectly worthy social goal. Using, in this case, a perfectly loony method.

It became clear to this prosecutor that Amanda had—why is this so hard for me to write?—fornicated.

Because, of course, Amanda was pregnant. When she was notified of the charges, Amanda said, "I didn't even know what fornication was. I had to look it up. It's any unmarried person who has sex, and they got me on that."

For her "crime," which resulted in the birth of an illicit bundle of joy named Tyler six days after she was sentenced in May, Amanda received a month of juvenile detention, suspended, plus three years' probation. She has also been ordered to stay in school, keep her waitressing job and attend parenting classes.

Personally, I would have pleaded religious miracle (if the star was lit, you must acquit), but the prosecutor also nabbed Amanda's partner in crime, her 16-year-old boyfriend, Chris Lay, whom she says she plans to marry after high school graduation.

"Ultimately," said a supporter of the prosecutions, "what we see in Emmett is going to be seen across the country."

And you thought the courts were already clogged.

The Problem of Teen Pregnancy

The problems of teen pregnancy are well recognized by now: They have become staples of political speeches about welfare reform, the crime rate, education. (Pick a social problem; teen pregnancy will be found somehow to exacerbate it.)

In the last couple of years, as well, it has become fashionable to talk about teen pregnancy in terms of the sexual exploitation of young women; according to the state Senate Office of Research, two-thirds of the babies born to California's teen mothers are fathered by men 20 and older. As a result, this state and many others are putting money and effort into the phenomenon seen in Idaho: renewed enforcement of old laws—in our case, statutory rape. California has dedicated more than $8 million to the enforcement of the statutory rape law in the last year, and according to news reports, this has resulted in nearly 300 convictions, up from practically none. Percentage-wise, not so great: the number of convictions represents about 1% of the estimated 30,000 babies born to teen mothers and adult fathers.

It's too early to tell whether prosecuting adult men on statutory rape charges will have the intended effect—that is,

---

District Attorney Views on Aggressive Enforcement of Statutory Rape Laws

A 1997 survey of 92 district attorneys in Kansas found that the majority favored aggressive enforcement of statutory rape laws. However, their opinions were mixed on whether prosecuting teens for statutory rape would reduce teen sex and teen pregnancy rates.

	Agree	Disagree	Neutral
Statutory rape laws should be aggressively enforced.	74%	6%	21%
Aggressive enforcement of statutory rape laws will reduce teen pregnancy.	24%	41%	35%
Aggressive enforcement of statutory rape laws will discourage teenagers from obtaining reproductive health care for fear of sexual partners being prosecuted.	17%	43%	39%

(Percentages may not equal 100% due to rounding.)

Henry L. Miller et al., *Family Planning Perspectives*, July/August 1998.

---

to put a crimp in the teen birthrate. Seems to me it might just give adult men a push in the direction of better contraception.

How will we prove their misdeeds then?

Prosecuting Teens Will Not Help

The Idaho prosecutions illustrate that, as always, punishment is the political path of least resistance when it comes to thorny social issues such as discouraging teens from having babies. Certainly, such prosecutions do nothing to encourage pregnant teens to seek help.

And nothing good ever comes from a teenager hiding a pregnancy.

Consider the case of a champion high school golfer in Oregon who has pleaded guilty to juvenile charges of criminally negligent homicide and concealing a birth. Kirsten Sundberg, now 18 and a college freshman, hid her pregnancy. Then, in November 1995, at 17, she gave birth to a baby at home in her bathroom as her parents slept. Seven weeks earlier, she had won a regional golf championship.

The baby, it was determined later, was born in a breech position and apparently suffocated during the birth. Her attorney said Kirsten thought the baby was born dead. She has not been accused of trying to harm the baby, and the prosecutor in her case plans to recommend probation when Kirsten is sentenced. . . .

Exactly what social goals are accomplished by these after-the-fact prosecutions is not clear. Wouldn't it make better sense, and accomplish more, to put our money and energy into sex education and contraception?

Amanda Smisek was prosecuted for having the nerve not to hide an unplanned pregnancy she brought to term; Kirsten Sundberg was prosecuted for the opposite reason.

Doesn't it seem that we are telling our teens, implicitly anyway, that abortion is the best solution to unwanted pregnancy? For some, it may be. For the rest, prosecution is hardly a sane alternative.

"*In most cases a parent's input is the best guarantee that a teenager will make a decision that is correct for her—be it abortion, adoption, or keeping the baby.*"

States Should Require Parental Notification Laws for Teen Abortions

Bruce A. Lucero

Bruce A. Lucero, a pro-choice family physician, argues that parental consent should be required before a minor girl can receive an abortion. He believes that a pregnant teen's parents are best suited to help her determine whether she should have an abortion, keep the baby, or give it up for adoption. Therefore, he concludes, it should be illegal to transport or accompany a minor across state lines for an abortion in order to evade state laws that require parental notification.

As you read, consider the following questions:

1. In the author's opinion, what reason do most teen girls give for not wanting to tell their parents about their pregnancies?
2. What are some of the risks a minor girl may face if she attempts to have an abortion without her parents' knowledge, according to Lucero?
3. Why do most people become pro-choice, in Lucer's view?

I am a doctor who performed some 45,000 abortions during 15 years in practice in Alabama. Even though I no longer perform abortions, I am still staunchly pro-choice.

But I find that I disagree with many in the pro-choice movement on the issue of parental notification laws for teenagers. Specifically, I support the Child Custody Protection bill. [The bill has not passed.] Under the legislation, it would be illegal for anyone to accompany a minor across state lines for an abortion if that minor failed to meet the requirement for parental consent or notification in her home state.

The legislation is important not only to the health of teen-age girls, but to the pro-choice movement as well.

Opponents of the measure believe that the bill would simply extend the reach of a state's parental notification or consent law to other states. And they claim that teen-agers would resort to unsafe abortions rather than tell their parents.

A Parent's Input

In truth, however, in most cases a parent's input is the best guarantee that a teen-ager will make a decision that is correct for her—be it abortion, adoption or keeping the baby. And it helps guarantee that if a teen-ager chooses an abortion, she will receive appropriate medical care.

In cases where teen-agers can't tell their parents—because of abuse, for instance—parental notification laws allow teen-agers to petition a judge for a waiver.

Society has always decided at what age teen-agers should have certain rights—be it the right to drive a car or the right to vote. In the same way, society should determine at what age a minor has the right to an abortion without notifying her parents.

In almost all cases, the only reason that a teen-age girl doesn't want to tell her parents about her pregnancy is that she feels ashamed and doesn't want to let her parents down.

But parents are usually the ones who can best help their teen-ager consider her options. And whatever the girl's decision, parents can provide the necessary emotional support and financial assistance. Even in a conservative state like Alabama, I found that parents were almost always supportive.

If a teen-ager seeks an abortion out of state, however,

things become infinitely more complicated. Instead of telling her parents, she may delay her abortion and try to scrape together enough money—usually $150 to $300—herself. As a result, she often waits too long and then has to turn to her parents for help to pay for a more expensive and riskier second-trimester abortion.

Parental Consent Required

How can we explain that in my hometown of Miami, Florida, my alma mater, Southwest High School, requires a parent to sign a release form, a permission slip, for a student to leave school grounds to attend even an educational and chaperoned field trip?

This same high school requires any student to obtain parental consent to receive mild medication such as aspirin in order to alleviate them of any discomfort they may experience during school hours.

In most schools, parents are given full notification of their children's educational choices; they are made aware that their children are enrolled in a basic sex education class and are given the option to withdraw them from the course.

These important rules and regulations are aimed at ensuring the safety of our children through parental guidance, yet somehow these same parents can be denied the right to know that their daughter was subjected to a secret and potentially fatal operation.

Ileana Ros-Lehitnen, Testimony before the Subcommittee on the Constitution, May 21, 1998.

Also, patients who receive abortions at out-of-state clinics frequently do not return for follow-up care, which can lead to dangerous complications. And a teen-ager who has an abortion across state lines without her parents' knowledge is even more unlikely to tell them that she is having complications.

Ultimately, the pro-choice movement hurts itself by opposing these kinds of laws. I have had many parents sit in my office with their teen-age daughter and say, "We never thought this would happen to us" or, "We were against abortion, but now it is different."

The hard truth is that people often become pro-choice only when they experience an unwanted pregnancy or when their daughter does. Too often, pro-choice advocates oppose laws that make common sense simply because the opposition supports or promotes them. The only way we can and should keep abortions legal is to keep them safe. To fight laws that would achieve this end does no one any good—not the pregnant teen-agers, the parents or the pro-choice movement.

> *"I always think now that I'd rather not know that my daughter had an abortion, if it meant that she could have the best of care, and come back home safely."*

States Should Not Require Parental Notification Laws for Teen Abortions

Bill Bell and Karen Bell

Several states have passed laws that require a minor girl's parents or a judge to be notified of her intent to have an abortion. In the following viewpoint, Bill Bell and Karen Bell of Indiana testify before a Congressional committee how their daughter Becky died from an illegal abortion because she was too frightened to tell them or a judge that she was pregnant. The Bells argue that their daughter Becky would still be alive if their family had lived in a state that permitted minors to receive confidential abortions without parental notification or consent. Therefore, they conclude, Congress should not make it illegal for an adult to transport a minor across state lines to receive an abortion without her parents' knowledge.

As you read, consider the following questions:

1. According to a Planned Parenthood counselor, why did Becky refuse to tell her family she was pregnant?
2. Why did Becky refuse to get a judicial bypass for an abortion, according to Planned Parenthood?
3. What percentage of teens tell their parents of their plans to have an abortion, as cited by the authors?

Reprinted from testimony given by Bill and Karen Bell on the Child Custody Protection Act, before the Subcommittee on the Constitution of the Committee on the Judiciary, May 20, 1998.

We appreciate the opportunity to appear before this committee today. I am Bill Bell, and alongside me is my wife Karen. We are here because of legislation that is being considered in Congress, the "Teen Endangerment Act." This legislation would make it a federal crime to transport a minor across state lines for the purpose of accessing an abortion. [The bill has not passed.]

Because of our daughter Becky's death from an illegal abortion, we have traveled the country speaking about teen pregnancy, abortion and parental involvement laws. We feel we can speak to these issues and laws with some knowledge and authority.

September of 1988 marks the 10th anniversary of our Becky's death. I would like for Karen to tell you our story.

Her Mother's Story

Do you remember when you were sixteen and fell in love for the first time? I remember when my daughter Becky was 16. She was our sunshine. Becky was my best friend. She had the kindest heart and loved old people, animals and babies.

Her brother Billy was 18 then, and we were planning to go on a family vacation. Every year, our family took a trip to Florida. That year, Becky seemed unhappy and I thought that our trip would make her feel better. But Becky didn't want to go. I know now that she was pregnant, and she came on the trip and we never knew that she was in trouble.

I found out after Becky's death that she had gone to a Planned Parenthood clinic—thank God for them, but they couldn't help Becky. The counselor who talked to Becky told us later that she wasn't afraid of us, that she loved us more than life itself. She was ashamed and didn't want to hurt the family.

The counselor asked Becky how old she was, and she said that she was 17. They told her that they couldn't help her because there was a law in Indiana that she had to tell her parents if she planned to have an abortion. They said, "Becky, you can go to Kentucky, 110 miles from here, where it's perfectly legal. Or, you can go to a judge to ask for a waiver." Becky said, "If I can't tell my mom and dad, how can I tell a judge who doesn't even know me?"

So on the Saturday night before her death the following Friday, September 16, 1988, she asked her father and I if she could go to a party on the south side of Indianapolis. She said that her friend was in trouble and needed her. I felt strange, that something wasn't right. My son Billy said, "Mom, let her go, she's been feeling unhappy and you protect her too much." It was difficult for me, but I listened to Billy and let her go.

It was about one o'clock in the morning and I heard her trying to get her key in the lock. I went to the door and I looked at her. Her hair was wet, she was crying, shaking, and I said, "What's wrong Becky?" And she said, "Mom, it was a bad party. Can I just go to bed?" I helped her get into bed and pulled the covers over her.

She Never Got Up Again

The next morning, she woke up with a stiff neck, very sick, and said that she had the flu, like her dad. Becky never lied, and so I believed her. She went to school the next day and was sick, we later found out, the whole day. When she got home from school she went to bed, and she never got up again.

On Wednesday, she was burning up with a high fever and a strange cough. Bill and I said, "You're going to have to go to the doctor." She gave us a terrified look, and said, "Please, Mom, don't make me go. Just give me some aspirin and I'll be OK." So we listened to her, but on Friday, at 11:00, she said "Mom, I'll go to the doctor now. See, I've started my period." She had actually started hemorrhaging, and we had no idea what had happened to her.

Her doctor took one look at her and told us that she had to go immediately to the hospital. We got back in the car and Dad put her in the backseat. I started to go around to the front seat, but she said, "Mom, will you sit in the backseat so I can lay my head on your shoulder?" I held her all the way to the hospital.

"I Love You, Mom and Dad"

When we got there, they put her in the pediatric ward, where she had always gone, since she was a little girl. The nuns and nurses knew her, and they asked her, "Becky, what have you done to yourself?" They couldn't draw blood; her veins had collapsed. She reverted back to being a little girl again, and asked for her Mom and Dad. I can remember she had her long, blond hair in a ponytail. I patted her head again. She took off her little love knot ring that she had always worn and handed it to me. She looked at her Dad and I, and said, "Forgive me for what I've done. I love you, Mom and Dad."

What's Wrong with Parental Notification or Consent Laws?

Parental notification or consent laws can expose a teenager from an abusive or otherwise dysfunctional family to emotional trauma and physical danger, and many young women who avoid telling their parents about their plans to terminate an unwanted pregnancy come from such families.

Courts have found that teenagers who want to keep their pregnancies a secret almost always have sound reasons. And family counseling experts have testified that forced communication frequently has disastrous results. Indeed, where abortion is concerned, privacy can be a life or death matter for teenagers.

Confidentiality has also proven crucial to the effective delivery to minors of several other health care services, including treatment for venereal disease and drug and alcohol abuse, prenatal care and contraception. Minors often shun such services if they fear that their privacy will not be respected. Thus, most states have passed laws *guaranteeing* a minor's right to receive confidential care in these areas.

American Civil Liberties Union, Briefing Paper Number 7, 1996.

That was the last time she ever talked to us again. Her heart stopped, and they took her away and told us to call the family. We called Billy at college, but he didn't get back in time to see her alive. As we were sitting in the small room, the doctor came in and said that he didn't know if he could save the baby. Bill and I had no idea what he was talking about.

At 11:29, they told us that her lungs had come apart. They took her off life support. They said they'd have to do an autopsy, because she had died less than 24 hours after being admitted. In the early morning, around 4 am, the phone rang and it was the coroner's office. Bill answered, and the coroner said, "Your Rebecca Suzanne died from an illegal, botched abortion. Dirty instruments were used on her." Bill told me, and I said, "Not Beck." She wouldn't hurt anyone or anything. Instead, she hurt herself.

I wanted to lie about her death. I told Bill we should just tell people at the funeral that she died of pneumonia. I didn't want people calling Becky names. So at the funeral, with all of our friends and Becky's school friends, the minister came down and knelt in front of us. He told us to tell the truth about what had happened. So we could hold ourselves up in the community. Billy reached over and took her hands, and said, "Mom, Dad, can I close the casket?" He patted Becky's head and said, "Nobody will ever hurt you again, Becky."

We went home, and I didn't care if I lived or died, neither did my husband. About six months went by, and Billy came to me one day and said, "I don't have a mom or dad anymore. My sister is buried a block away. I'm 19 and I'm scared and I've lost my whole family. Why don't you tell the truth that we were a good family. Tell others what happened to my sister so that this won't happen to other families."

The parental consent law in Indiana was responsible for Becky's death. It didn't make her come to her dad and I. The thing that makes me sick to this day is that I would have voted for that law. Because every parent would want to know if their child was in trouble. I always think now that I'd rather not know that my daughter had an abortion, if it meant that she could have the best of care, and come back home safely.

Her Father's Story

Many of you may have daughters or granddaughters, and I am sure that you would want to be involved in any issues relating to their health and well being. Just as Karen and I did. Yet, the law in Indiana that required a parent's consent did not force Becky to involve us at her most desperate time.

Studies tell us that between 60–70 percent of the teens who have abortions each year will involve their parents in making the decision whether or not to have an abortion. And if you think about it, these restrictive laws have no impact on their decision. Where we would like to focus attention is the 30–40 percent of teens who for whatever reason, cannot involve their parents. These are the young women who are punished by these laws. Yes, we want very much for our daughters to involve us, but once they make the decision, this law being considered will not force these young women to involve their parents. Are we willing to sacrifice any of our young women so that the proponents of these laws can have their way?

How can we ignore what we know to be true, that there are young women who will go to any extreme to avoid involving their parents? Is it acceptable for us to force them into acts of desperation? Young women are committing suicide, self-inducing and going to the back alleys, rather than going to their parents.

I would ask you, have you ever taken the time to just talk to our young people, and young women in particular? I realize that they don't vote, therefore they have no voice. My wife and I have talked to many young women, and it is very clear to us that there are young women who would do anything to avoid having to tell their parents. Would it not be in the best interest of these young women to have access to safe health care, rather than forcing them into life-endangering acts?

Had the Bell family lived 100 miles to the south, our Becky would be alive today, but like many young women she didn't have the transportation to go where she would have a safe, legal abortion. In her desperation she chose to go to some back alley and her fate was determined there.

As Karen and I considered coming to Washington again, to speak out against this dangerous legislation, we thought of our 2-month-old granddaughter. Someday she will be 17. We realized we'd do everything possible to ensure that she will have options her Aunt Becky did not.

I would just like to finish by saying: The law in Indiana did not make Becky come to us. Will this law be any different?

"A baby is not such a bad reason for marriage; marriages taken to legitimate a pregnancy are no less stable on average than other marriages."

Unwed Teen Parents Should Be Encouraged to Marry

Maggie Gallagher

In the following viewpoint, Maggie Gallagher argues that while the teen pregnancy rate has not changed since the 1970s, the number of teens who are bearing children out of wedlock has increased dramatically. This rise in unwed motherhood is due to a national campaign against teen marriage, she maintains, in which society bombards teenagers with the message that they are too young to marry. Unfortunately, Gallagher contends, unwed mothers are less likely to marry at all or achieve their other goals. Therefore, she asserts, society should emphasize marriage for pregnant teens. Gallagher is the author of *The Abolition of Marriage: How We Destroy Lasting Love* and a scholar affiliated with the Institute of American Values, a family and social policy research organization.

As you read, consider the following questions:
1. How much more likely is it that a single pregnant teen will choose unwed motherhood over marriage in the 1990s than in the 1970s, according to the author?
2. How does one health textbook refer to married teens, as cited by Gallagher?
3. What percentage of marriages among older teens survive, according to Gallagher?

Reprinted from "Campaign Against Teen Marriage," by Maggie Gallagher, *Conservative Chronicle*, October 6, 1999. Reprinted with permission from Universal Press Syndicate.

What is the cause of today's teen pregnancy crisis? In absolute terms, the number of teen women having their first child is no larger now than in the early '70s. The big change is not in teens' fertility behavior but in their marital behavior: Today, a single, pregnant teen is three times more likely to pick unwed motherhood over marriage as she was in the early '70s. White teen mothers are only about one-sixth as likely to choose adoption today as they were a generation ago.

Scholars and policy makers have torn their hair out trying to explain these errant young women's inexplicable desire to mother. Are they deformed by a culture of poverty? Are they seduced by a culture of welfare? Are they a product of a nation defining deviancy downward?

The National Campaign Against Teen Marriage

To all these explanations I would add, after an intensive study of early, unwed childbearing for *The Age of Unwed Mothers*, a new, overlooked possibility: In preferring unwed motherhood over early marriage, today's young women are not so much rebelling against social norms as obediently conforming to adult advice. The national campaign against teen marriage has been more powerful than the national campaign against teen pregnancy.

And campaign is not too strong a word to describe experts' hostility toward early marriage for pregnant women, despite an extremely limited amount of research on the question. Even today, health textbooks in high schools issue dire warnings that teen marriage "can be disastrous," as a 1996 text put it, transforming teens into "social outcasts."

Not a single current health textbook I reviewed treated marriage as favorably as unwed childbearing (for pregnant teens); no textbook suggested that young pregnant couples who married could use pluck, commitment and social support (as unwed mothers were urged) to overcome the inherent difficulties of young marriage.

Is marriage really a fate worse than unwed motherhood? Probably not. For example, contrary to popular lore, a baby is not such a bad reason for marriage; marriages taken to legitimate a pregnancy are no less stable on average than other marriages. Teen marriages are more likely to fail, but about half of marriages among older teens survive (compared to about 70 percent of marriages in which the bride is at least 23 years old).

Marriage and Family Are Connected

In interviews with young unwed mothers, Maggie Gallagher often heard the refrain: "I'd like to marry eventually, but I'm still too young." Old enough to assume the heavy responsibilities of motherhood, but too young to marry?

It appears we must address profound deficiencies in the way we talk to young people about marriage and the family. Increasingly, our youth seem to be picking up the message that while marriage may demand maturity, parenting does not; and that marriage and children are totally separate and unrelated spheres of life.

Dana Mack, *Los Angeles Times*, October 4, 1999.

Moreover, when young mothers fail to marry the father of their child, they may never marry at all. In one large, national study, unwed mothers were just as likely to want marriage but only half as likely to succeed in getting married as childless young women. These researchers conclude that "it seems women generally are not having children nonmaritally as a response to poor marriage prospect. Rather, having a child outside of marriage appears to derail young women's existing plans."

Worth Waiting For

Marriage is not a good bet for every pregnant young woman. But by bringing a marriage focus back to teen pregnancy programs, we make it more likely that the next generation of single women will do a variety of useful things: abstain from sex, contracept faithfully, avoid men who aren't good marriage material, and in cases when marriage isn't advisable, consider giving a baby a married home through adoption.

The reason today's young women do less of all these things is intimately related to what adults are saying (and not saying) about teen pregnancy. Why wait to have a baby until another birthday rolls around? Will it really make that big a difference whether you become a single mother at 19 or 20?

To be really effective, a new national campaign will have to abandon the misconception that our problem is primarily "children having children" and work to pass on to the next generation this key idea: Marriage—the gift of loving partner and committed father—is the thing worth waiting for.

> *"For young parents who have little knowledge of how to raise children well, getting married, by itself, will not solve the difficulties their children face."*

Teen Marriages Are Not Always Beneficial

Melissa Ludtke

Pregnant girls were less likely to get married in the 1990s than their peers in the 1960s. In the following viewpoint, Melissa Ludtke maintains that marriage does not make economic sense for many teens who are expecting to become parents. Furthermore, she contends, being married does not necessarily make the baby's mother a better parent. Instead of telling teens they are too young to marry, Ludtke argues that society should persuade teens that they are too young to be parents. Ludtke, a former writer for *Time* magazine, is the author of *On Our Own: Unmarried Motherhood in America*.

As you read, consider the following questions:

1. How many new adolescent mothers are there every year, according to Ludtke?
2. According to the author, what percentage of teen mothers were unwed in 1997 compared to 1960?
3. What type of essential support do many unwed teen mothers receive from their families, according to Ludtke?

S he was 17 years old, six months pregnant with her second child, and living in public housing in Boston with the 21-year-old man who is the father. She had earned a Graduate Equivalency Degree. Her boyfriend hadn't, nor had he finished high school or secured a job. Did she intend to marry the father of her children?

"Get married? Never," she told me. Like most of the dozens of teen-age mothers I interviewed from 1992 to 1995, this young woman was raised in a poor and fractured family and community. Her mother and father were not married; her mother's first husband was an alcoholic. The second husband, the young woman said, had tried to sexually abuse her. Her mother was unwilling to protect her, she claimed, so at 15, she left home. Soon she became pregnant.

An Increase in Out-of-Wedlock Births

Like most adolescent mothers—and there are half a million new ones each year—she was aimless, failing in school, feeling abandoned. She saw having a baby as giving her someone to belong to and something to be.

Though the rate of births to teen-age mothers has declined significantly since the 1950's, out-of-wedlock births to adolescents are way up: 76 percent of teen-age mothers are not married, compared with 15 percent in 1960. The 1996 welfare law offers a bonus of $20 million apiece to the five states that show the greatest two-year decline in out-of-wedlock births.

There was a time, not very long ago, when it made sense for teen-agers who were about to become parents to get married, even though many such marriages didn't last. Young men who hadn't finished high school could find steady jobs with decent wages, work that provided some benefits for families. There were also fewer expectations for women. If a teen-ager abandoned her education to become a wife and mother—as many did—most people considered that trade-off acceptable.

But today the employment prospects for poorly educated young men are dim. When men can't provide for a family, they are less likely to get married. And when teen-age mothers marry, many end up abandoning their own education. A lot of the young mothers I spoke with told me that if they had married the father of their child, he would have insisted they leave school to devote their full energies to him and the child.

The Revival of "Shotgun" Marriage

Even at 13, the most vulnerable girls may see men and motherhood as the best of their limited options. And they are already on the way to motherhood. . . .

Statutory rape laws are based on the notion that a girl below a certain age isn't mature enough to legally consent to sex. How, then, is she old enough to consent to marriage? Do we only care that a girl is unwed? Or that she is unprotected?

Ellen Goodman, *Liberal Opinion Week*, September 23, 1996.

Adolescent mothers often receive essential support from family members—guidance and assistance that enables them to stay in school, learn how to be better parents, and prepare for employment. Some of them would lose that support if they got married and moved out. Also, a young mother's family often views her in a different way once she is married, expecting her and her husband to be self-sufficient.

Maturity

Would marriage mean that a poorly educated teen-age mother would read to her children? Not necessarily. Would marriage mean that a very young mother wouldn't become overwhelmed by her responsibilities and harshly discipline her child? No. It is important for a child to have both parents present. But for young parents who have little knowledge of how to raise children well, getting married, by itself, will not solve the difficulties their children face.

Most of the young mothers I visited said they were ready to be mothers, but not wives. They got it half right. Being a wife isn't something an adolescent girl should take on. Our job is to help them, and their boyfriends, understand why they are not ready to be parents, either.

Periodical Bibliography

The following articles have been selected to supplement the diverse views presented in this chapter. Addresses are provided for periodicals not indexed in the *Readers' Guide to Periodical Literature*, the *Alternative Press Index*, the *Social Sciences Index*, or the *Index to Legal Periodicals and Books*.

Ethan Bronner	"Lawsuit on Sex Bias by 2 Mothers, 17," *New York Times*, August 6, 1998.
James Brooke	"Idaho County Finds Way to Chastise Pregnant Teen-Agers: They Go to Court," *New York Times*, October 28, 1996.
Catherine Elton	"Jail Baiting," *New Republic*, October 20, 1997.
Linda Feldman	"Targeting Boys in Fight Against Teen Pregnancy," *Christian Science Monitor*, January 7, 1998.
Elizabeth Gleick	"Putting the Jail in Jailbait," *Time*, January 29, 1996.
Elisha Dov Hack	"College Life vs. My Moral Code," *New York Times*, September 9, 1997.
Quentin Hardy	"Idaho County Tests a New Way to Curb Teen Sex: Prosecute," *Wall Street Journal*, July 8, 1996.
Michael Lynch	"Enforcing 'Statutory Rape'?" *Public Interest*, Summer 1998.
Bobbie Ann Mason	"Shame, Honor, and High School," *New York Times*, August 13, 1998.
Kristin A. Moore	"Welfare Bill Won't Stop Teen-Age Pregnancy," *Christian Science Monitor*, December 18, 1995.
Ellen Perlman	"The Mother of All Welfare Problems," *Governing*, January 1997.
Politics and the Life Sciences	Symposium on Adolescent Sexuality and Public Policy, September 1996.
William J. Sneck	"Premarital Divorce," *America*, November 15, 1997.

CHAPTER 4

What Should Teens Be Taught About Sex?

Chapter Preface

In 1996, concern over the high teen pregnancy rate led Congress to include legislation in its Welfare Reform Act allocating $50 million over five years to states that agree to teach abstinence-only education programs in the nation's public schools. Schools that accept the funds must instruct students that "abstinence from sexual activity is the only certain way to avoid out-of-wedlock pregnancy, sexually transmitted diseases, and other associated health problems." To ensure that students receive the abstinence-only message, the legislation prohibits schools from using the grant money to teach students about contraceptives or how to protect themselves from sexually transmitted diseases.

Advocates of the abstinence-only program contend that teaching students to say "no" to sex is the most effective way to reduce the teen sex and teen pregnancy rates and to reduce the spread of sexually transmitted diseases (STDs). According to Elayne Bennett, founder of the national abstinence program Best Friends, students are given a mixed message when they are told to be chaste until marriage yet receive instructions in birth control and how to prevent STDs. In fact, proponents of abstinence-only education claim their programs are responsible for the 17 percent decline in the teen pregnancy rate from 1990 to 1996.

While most sex education experts agree that students should be taught the value of abstinence, some believe that abstinence-only programs are fear-based and ineffective at reducing the teen sex and teen pregnancy rates. Douglas J. Kirby, a sex education researcher, studied abstinence-only programs and concluded "the five published evaluations of abstinence-only programs did not find a delay in the onset of sexual intercourse." Furthermore, Debra Haffner, president of the Sexuality Information and Education Council of the United States, argues, "Denying them information about contraceptives and STD protections puts them at risk."

In the following chapter, sex education experts examine the morality and effectiveness of abstinence-only and comprehensive sex education programs.

"The best that 'safer sex' approaches can offer is some risk reduction. Abstinence, on the other hand, offers risk elimination."

Abstinence-Only Programs Reduce Teen Sexual Activity

Joe S. McIlhaney Jr.

Joe S. McIlhaney Jr. is a gynecologist and president of the Medical Institute for Sexual Health, an organization he founded in 1992 to educate the public about the issues of nonmarital pregnancy and sexually transmitted diseases. In the following viewpoint, McIlhaney argues that sexually active teens have a high risk of becoming pregnant and of contracting sexually transmitted diseases. Sex education programs that teach "safer sex" methods of contraception are ineffective at reducing teen sexual activity, he asserts. In his opinion, the only certain way to reduce and eliminate the risks of sexual activity is to teach teens to practice abstinence until marriage.

As you read, consider the following questions:

1. Why do teens and young adults have the highest risk for contracting sexually transmitted diseases, according to the author?
2. How effective are condoms against the human papilloma virus, as cited by McIlhaney?
3. In the author's opinion, what is the "bottom line" about "safer sex" approaches to teen sexual activity?

Abstinence. What's so controversial? Parents, educators and communities want teenagers to postpone becoming sexually active, preferably until marriage, because the risks of sexual activity in the nineties simply are too high, right? Everyone agrees that teen pregnancy and sexually transmitted diseases, or STDs, including HIV, cause serious problems. But how to prevent these problems and educate our young people—that is controversial.

We have had at least 20 years of an educational message that says, basically, "If you can't say no, act responsibly." Yet these safe/safer/protected sex curricula have been tried and found wanting in terms of preventing the skyrocketing damage to our teens and their long-term physical, emotional, social, spiritual and economic health.

It is time for an honest and open-minded look at a new sexual revolution: abstinence until a committed, lifelong, mutually monogamous relationship. Most people call it marriage.

The Risks of Sexual Activity

Are the problems associated with sexual activity really all that bad? You might be surprised. The data are startling. Here are just a few sound bites:

- One million teenage girls become pregnant each year.
- One in 10 females between the ages 15 and 19 become pregnant each year.
- Seventy-two percent of the resulting babies are born out of wedlock.
- Three million teenagers acquire an STD each year.
- One in four sexually active teenagers acquires a new STD each year.
- Two-thirds of all people who acquire STDs are under age 25.
- Eight new STD "germs" have been identified since 1980, including HIV.
- One-quarter of all new HIV infections are found in people under age 22.
- Of all diseases that are required to be reported in the United States, 87 percent are STDs (1995 data).

Nonmarital teen pregnancy all too often has a devastating impact on teen parents and their children. Indeed, teen pregnancy has received much analysis because of the long-term effects not only to the mother and child, but to the father, to extended families and ultimately to society. *Kids Having Kids*, a 1996 report from the Robin Hood Foundation, reveals that only 30 percent of girls who become pregnant before age 18 will earn a high-school diploma by the age of 30, compared with 76 percent of women who delay child bearing until after age 20. And 80 percent of those young, single mothers will live below the poverty line, receive welfare and raise children who are at risk for many difficulties as they grow to adulthood.

Adolescent dads also do not progress as far educationally and earn, on average, about $2,000 less annually at age 27 as a direct result of the impact of teen parenthood.

One other concern surrounding teen pregnancy often is overlooked. Studies from the California Department of Health Services found that 77 percent of the babies born to girls in high school were fathered by men older than high-school age. For girls in junior high, the father was, on average, 6.5 years older. These studies highlight the problem that a substantial portion of teenage sexual activity is more a matter of manipulation, coercion or abuse than anything else.

Sexually Transmitted Diseases

In addition to pregnancy, adolescents and young adults are in the age group at highest risk for contracting STDs. Why? Here are two reasons. First, teenage reproductive systems are not yet mature. That is why, for instance, the risk of pelvic inflammatory disease, or PID, is as much as 10 times greater for a 15-year-old sexually active female than for a 24-year-old. PID usually is caused by STDs such as gonorrhea or chlamydia, which often have no noticeable symptoms. PID is the most rapidly increasing cause of infertility in the United States today.

The second reason that teens are at higher risk for STDs is behavioral. The two leading factors associated with STD infection are how early in life someone begins to have sex and the number of different sexual partners someone has. The Centers for Disease Control and Prevention, or CDC, has reported that by 12th grade, 18 percent of students already have had four or more sexual partners—that's almost one in five high-school seniors. With each additional sexual partner, the odds of acquiring an STD increase significantly.

We all are aware of the devastating and fatal consequences of HIV and AIDS. But other STDs have serious, even life-threatening, consequences. Some STDs can cause scarring in reproductive organs, causing infertility. Others can cause pregnancy or birth complications, including birth defects. And having one STD can make a person more susceptible to acquiring others, even HIV. Hepatitis B can lead to cirrhosis of the liver or liver cancer. And human papilloma virus, or HPV, the cause of genital warts, has been linked to cancers of the cervix, penis, anus and vulva. In fact, more women die of cervical cancer (nearly 5,000 annually) than die of AIDS-related diseases. More than 90 percent of all cervical cancer is caused by HPV.

One additional fact: Condoms provide virtually no protection from HPV, even when used correctly. That's right! Condoms do not protect against HPV because this virus is passed via skin to skin contact and (have you noticed?) condoms do not cover everything.

The Controversy

The statistics for disease and pregnancy are not in dispute. The concern is in what we should do about preventing these problems from occurring and devastating young lives. This is where the controversy starts.

The prevailing opinion for the last two or three decades has been that "kids will do it anyway, so we have to give them condoms and contraceptives so they can be protected." Education programs have given a nod to abstinence as the only 100 percent safe choice outside of marriage but then have gone on to spend much time and emphasis on the "how to's" of "safer" sex. The failure rates of contraception and condoms are not emphasized due to concern that these facts might discourage kids from using them.

The bottom line is that although studies show that "safer sex" approaches do not increase sexual activity among students, none of these programs has dramatically lowered the number of teens who choose to be sexually active, who have to deal with pregnancy or who acquire STDs. Nor have they

Teaching Style for Sex Education

Non-Directive:

• Teacher's principle role is as Facilitator.

• Knowledge is aimed at awareness.

• Knowledge is key—more information and awareness given to the student.

• Sex education is taught without moral distinctions.

• Affective—Emotions, opinions, feelings predominate.

• Public classrooms are not the appropriate place to give directions for expected behavior.

• Decision making skills encourage young people to consider all options, enable and encourage youth to make "appropriate" decisions.

• Over-emphasis on non-judgmental attitudes.

• Contraceptives discussed with emphasis on use; failure rates downplayed. Little emotional distress discussed.

• Most teens will be sexually active, and the best that adults can hope for is that they will act "responsibly."

• Abstinence is presented as a choice.

Directive:

• Teacher is Director giving guidelines, standards, and reasons.

• Knowledge is aimed at prevention.

• Knowledge alone is not enough—clear direction must be given.

• A clear message is always given. No "neutral" position.

• Effective—Truth predominates.

• The classroom may be the only place some teens are ever exposed to *expected standards of behavior.*

• Decision-making skills which lead young people to make good healthy decisions are taught.

• Judgments of behavior, not persons.

• Risks, diseases, emotional distress, and failure rates of contraceptives are discussed.

• Most teens do abstain while many others respond to "Secondary Virginity" and start over again.

• Abstinence is presented as the goal.

Onalee McGraw, Educational Guidance Institute, 1991.

dramatically increased contraceptive use among those who are sexually active.

Even so, isn't it important to promote the use of condoms in school? Let's look at the facts. In the long run, condoms only work when used every time and used correctly. Also, as pointed out earlier, even when used perfectly they provide little, if any, protection from some STDs.

The highest rates of perfect condom use have been reported in two major studies of couples who knew one partner was infected with HIV. In both of these studies only about 50 percent of the participating couples managed perfect condom use during a two-year period. If this is the best these couples could do, even when they knew they were at risk for a potentially fatal disease, imagine the probability of teens using condoms consistently and correctly over the duration of their premarital years.

Research studies vary widely, due to different methodologies and populations, but in any case the news on consistency of teen condom use is not good. Some studies have found that as few as 5 percent of sexually active teens consistently use condoms, and even the most optimistic have found that only 40 percent do. When given a standard set of instructions to which to refer, no more than 50 percent of adolescents typically report that they use condoms correctly. A CDC study found that only half of sexually active high-school students used a condom the last time they had sex. They also found that 25 percent of sexually active teens used drugs or alcohol at the time of their last sexual experience. This, of course, lessens still further any chance that barrier protection was used correctly, if at all. Critics claim that teaching abstinence is "unrealistic," but it is certainly no more unrealistic than expecting teens to achieve ideal condom usage.

Why should abstinence be emphasized in schools? The best that "safer sex" approaches can offer is some risk reduction. Abstinence, on the other hand, offers risk elimination. When the risks of pregnancy and disease are so great, even with contraception, how can we advocate anything less?

There are a lot of sexual-lifestyle options in our society today, but they are not all equally healthy. Schools should promote what is healthy for students. They should set the standard. When standards are low, students will achieve at mediocre levels. They will achieve at higher levels when standards are set at levels that are realistic, but high.

Some students will continue to be sexually active. We need to deal with them with sensitivity and care. But many other students will choose a healthier lifestyle when encouraged in that direction. If students who are sexually active use condoms, they may gain some risk reduction. But they must not leave the sex-education classroom thinking, "I'm being responsible and safe if I use a condom." The school's message must be unmistakably clear: "There is no responsible sex for unmarried teenagers."

Is teaching abstinence realistic? You bet. Let me highlight just one approach: the young women involved in the Best Friends program, founded in Washington 10 years ago. Beginning in the fifth grade and continuing through high school, girls are provided adult mentors, fun activities and social support for abstaining from sex, drugs and alcohol and finishing their education. The focus is on freedom for the future gained by delaying what might feel good now but damages lives later. A 1995 study found that girls in the Best Friends program had a 1.1 percent pregnancy rate, compared with a 26 percent rate for teen girls in the Washington area.

The New Sexual Revolution

This is the new sexual revolution. The current risks and later regrets are potentially too profound to offer our young people any less than the opportunity to have the very best choice emphasized, explained and encouraged. To present "protected" sex as an alternative to abstinence is inadequate. Waiting for sexual freedom within marriage isn't an easy goal, but the alternative of broken hearts and broken lives from disease or pregnancy makes this a goal worth establishing. We owe it to our teens to tell the truth, to set the standard and to give them our full support toward a healthy future.

> "*There are* no *published studies in the professional literature indicating that abstinence-only programs will result in young people delaying intercourse.*"

Abstinence-Only Programs Are Ineffective

Debra W. Haffner

In the following viewpoint, Debra W. Haffner argues that comprehensive sex education programs are more effective in preventing teen pregnancies and sexually transmitted diseases than fear-based abstinence-only sex education programs. She maintains that more than half of American teenagers have had sexual intercourse, a percentage that has remained unchanged since 1990. Federal guidelines requiring schools to teach abstinence-only sex education programs will not reduce the number of sexually active teens, she contends. Therefore, Haffner asserts, teenagers need information and access to contraceptives in order to grow into healthy, responsible adults. Haffner is the president and chief executive officer of the Sexuality Information and Education Council of the United States.

As you read, consider the following questions:

1. According to the World Health Organization, which programs are most effective in changing teen sexual behaviors?
2. What was the average age of first intercourse for teen males and females in the 1950s and '60s as compared to the 1970s and '80s, as cited by Haffner?

Reprinted with permission from "What's Wrong with Abstinence-Only Sexuality Education Programs?" by Debra W. Haffner, *SIECUS Report*, April/May 1997.

The Sexuality Information and Education Council of the United States (SIECUS) supports abstinence. I repeat. SIECUS supports abstinence. But SIECUS does not support teaching young people *only* about abstinence.

SIECUS's *Guidelines for Comprehensive Sexuality Education: Kindergarten–12th Grade* state that one of the four primary goals of comprehensive education is "to help young people exercise responsibility regarding sexual relationships, including addressing abstinence and [how] to resist pressures to become prematurely involved in sexual relationships."

Abstinence is one of the 36 topics covered in the *Guidelines*, and messages about abstinence are included in age-appropriate sections.

SIECUS does *not* believe in abstinence-only approaches to sexuality education that have as "their exclusive purpose teaching the social, psychological, and health gains to be realized by abstaining from sexual activity." (This is what the newly funded $50 million federal program will require grant recipients to teach American youth.)

SIECUS does, however, support programs that are abstinence-based—such as *Postponing Sexual Involvement* and *Will Power, Won't Power*—that provide young people with clear messages about abstaining in the context of a broader, more comprehensive program.

An Ineffective Program

Abstinence-only sexuality education is not effective. Proponents of such sexuality education make broad claims that sound exciting. They argue that if you tell young people to abstain from sexual intercourse, they will. These "just say no" programs promise to keep young people from developing "too serious" relationships, from being emotionally hurt, from experimenting with intimacy and sexual behaviors, and, of course, from getting pregnant and from contracting an STD or HIV.

There is no reason to believe that these claims are true. There are *no* published studies in the professional literature indicating that abstinence-only programs will result in young people delaying intercourse. In fact, a recent $5 million abstinence-only initiative in California not only did not increase the number of young people who abstained, but, in one school, actually resulted in more students having sexual intercourse after having participated in the course. Proponents of abstinence-only fear-based programs often recite their own in-house evaluations as proof that these programs are effective. Yet, they have not published their evaluations in peer reviewed literature and are not willing to make them available for review by outside researchers.

The Benefits of a Comprehensive Sex Ed Program

Comprehensive sexuality education is, on the other hand, an effective strategy for giving young people the skills to delay their involvement in sexual behaviors. Several reviews of published evaluations of sexuality education, HIV prevention, and teenage pregnancy prevention programs have consistently found that:

• sexuality education does not encourage teens to start having sexual intercourse or to increase their frequency of sexual intercourse.

• programs must take place before young people begin experimenting with sexual behaviors if they are to result in a delay of sexual intercourse.

• teenagers who start having intercourse following a sexuality education program are more likely to use contraceptives than those who have not participated in a program.

• HIV programs that use cognitive and behavioral skills training with adolescents demonstrate "consistently positive" results.

Indeed, a recent World Health Organization review of 35 studies found that the programs most effective in changing young people's behavior are those that address abstinence, contraception, *and* STD prevention. In addition, the National Institutes of Health's Consensus Panel on AIDS said in February 1997 that the abstinence-only approach to sexuality education "places policy in direct conflict with science and ignores overwhelming evidence that other programs [are] effective."

Fear-based, abstinence-only programs also fail to address many of the antecedents of early first intercourse. Extensive research conducted during the past two decades has clearly delineated a portrait of a young person who begins intercourse prior to age 14.

Education programs cannot influence some of the factors such as early physical development, lower age of menarche or a higher testosterone level, older siblings, single-parent household environments, or mothers with lower educational attainment.

Sexuality education programs can, however, potentially address other factors such as young people's perception of their friends' and siblings' sexual behaviors, the timing of first dating, steady relationships, and beliefs about gender role stereotypes.

Other venues such as counseling and mentoring programs can address these other antecedents of early first intercourse: lower school performance, lower reading and writing skills, lack of parental support, lower church attendance, depression, and other problem behaviors, such as substance use (including alcohol and nicotine), and school delinquency.

Federal Requirement #1

The new welfare reform program requires that sexuality education classes in the United States teach that "abstinence from sexual activity outside marriage is the expected standard for all school-age children." Although adults may very well want this as a standard, it is far from accurate in describing the reality of today's teenagers.

Almost all American adolescents engage in some type of sexual behavior. Although most policy debates about sexuality education have focused on sexual intercourse and its negative consequences, young people actually explore their sexuality from a much wider framework that includes dating, relationships, and intimacy.

The welfare reform legislation never even defines "sexual activity." Since the definition includes the word "activity" rather than "intercourse," one must assume that it is broader and includes a prohibition against other activities besides sexual intercourse. This is, however, never stated. For clarification, the Medical Institute for Sexual Health (MISH) defines *abstinence* as "avoiding sexual intercourse as well as any genital contact or genital stimulation." Other fear-based curricula define it as any behaviors beyond hand holding and light kissing.

The reality is that sexual behavior is almost universal among American adolescents. A majority of American teenagers date, over 85 percent have had a boyfriend or girlfriend and have kissed someone romantically, and nearly 80 percent have engaged in deep kissing.

A Sorry Mess

The record of abstinence-only programs is a sorry mess. Douglas Kirby, a nationally recognized expert on sex education, told Scripps Howard News Service that an abstinence-only program in California public schools called Postponing Sexual Involvement (one of the few in the country that does not also teach kids about birth control) had no impact on the pregnancy rate of teens who took part in it. In fact, Postponing Sexual Involvement's impact seems to have boomeranged, as California's teen pregnancy rate is the highest in the nation.

Bonnie Erbe, *Washington Times*, April 5, 1997.

The majority of young people move from kissing to more intimate sexual behaviors during their teenage years. More than 50 percent engage in "petting behaviors." By the age of 14, more than 50 percent of all boys have touched a girl's breasts, and 25 percent have touched a girl's vulva. By the age of 18, more than 75 percent have engaged in heavy petting. From 25 to 50 percent of teens report that they have experienced fellatio and/or cunnilingus. A recent study found that of those teens who are virgins, nearly one third reported that they had engaged in heterosexual masturbation of or by a partner. One tenth of virgins had participated in oral sex, and one percent had participated in anal intercourse.

More than half of American teenagers in schools have had sexual intercourse. The latest data from the Youth Risk Behavior Surveillance System of the U.S. Centers for Disease Control and Prevention found that 54 percent of high school students had sexual intercourse, a rate virtually unchanged since the study began in 1990. By the time they reach the age of 20, 80 percent of boys and 76 percent of girls have had sexual intercourse.

At each stage of adolescence, higher proportions of boys and girls have had sexual intercourse today than 20 years ago. The largest increase occurred between 1971 and 1979. The increase was modest in the 1980s. It appeared to level off in the 1990s. It is important to note, however, that these trends started much earlier than the 1970s. In fact, the modal age for first intercourse was 17 for men and 18 for women in the 1950s and 1960s. It was 16 for men and nearly 17 for women in the 1970s and 1980s. This is a one-year change over a 40-year span.

Federal Requirement #2

The new federal program also requires that grantees teach that "abstinence from sexual activity is the only certain way to avoid out-of-wedlock pregnancy, sexually transmitted diseases, and other associated health problems."

On the surface, it is hard to argue with this statement. The SIECUS *Guidelines* themselves state that "abstinence from sexual intercourse is the most effective method of preventing pregnancies and STDS/HIV." Yet, after learning that abstinence is the "only certain way" to avoid pregnancy and STDS/HIV, young people may get the impression that contraception and condoms are not effective. In fact, many of the fear-based approaches to sexuality education discuss methods of contraception only in terms of their failure rates. Indeed, professionals who work directly with adolescents in schools and clinics can attest that adolescent vows of abstinence fail far more than condoms do.

Messages that contraception and condoms are not effective could, unfortunately, reverse the significant strides that American youth have made toward having safer sex during the past two decades. Consider these statistics:

• In 1979, fewer than 50 percent of adolescents used a contraceptive at first intercourse.

• In 1988, more than 65 percent used them.

• By 1990, more than 70 percent used them.

Teenagers who receive contraceptive education in the same year that they become sexually active are 70 to 80 percent more likely to use contraceptive methods (including condoms) and more than twice as likely to use the pill.

Abstinence-Plus

Public arguments about the sexual education of teens tend to mix up the issues of what are appropriate moral lessons to give them, and what works best in preventing teens from getting pregnant.

If what you care about is teen pregnancy, the data suggest the programs that work best combine abstinence messages with contraception as a backup. "What a large majority of American sexuality educators and a large majority of Americans are pushing for is abstinence-plus," sex researcher Douglas Kirby says.

This means "you give real weight to abstinence, you give it serious attention, you say that abstinence is the only method that is 100 percent effective against pregnancy and sexually transmitted diseases. But then you also talk about condoms and contraception in a balanced and accurate manner."

E.J. Dionne Jr., *San Diego Union Tribune*, July 16, 1999.

It is vitally important that programs encourage young people who engage in intercourse to use contraception and condoms. According to the National Institutes of Health, "although sexual abstinence is a desirable objective, programs must include instruction in safe sex behavior, including condom use."

Federal Requirement #3

The new abstinence-only programs must also teach that "a mutually faithful monogamous relationship in the context of marriage is the expected standard of human sexual activity."

This "information" is clearly not true in American culture. The fact is that the vast majority of Americans begin having sexual relationships (including sexual intercourse) as teenagers. Fewer than 7 percent of men and 20 percent of women aged 18 to 59 were virgins when they were married. Only 10 percent of adult men and 22 percent of adult women report that their first sexual experience was with their spouse, many of whom had their first intercourse when they were engaged prior to marriage. Indeed, this "norm" was probably never true: a third of all Pilgrim brides were pregnant when they were married.

There are currently more than 74 million American adults who are classified as single because they have delayed marriage, decided to remain single, are divorced, or have entered into a gay or lesbian partnership. More than three quarters of these men and two thirds of these women have had sex with a partner in the past 12 months. Most of them would take offense at this new "standard of human behavior." Under this new program's definition, schools will teach young people that these adults must remain celibate throughout their lives.

The concept of chastity until marriage may have made more sense a hundred years ago when teenagers reached puberty in their middle teens. For them, marriage and other adult responsibilities closely followed. Today's young people are different: They reach puberty earlier, they have intercourse earlier, and they marry in their middle twenties. In fact, women and men marry several years later today than they did in the 1950s. The current mean age for first marriage is 26.7 years old for men and 24.5 years old for women.

Federal Requirement #4

The new federal programs must also teach that "sexual activity outside of marriage is likely to have harmful psychological and physical effects."

There is no sound public health data to support this statement. It is certainly true that sexual relations can lead to unplanned pregnancies, STDS, and HIV. It is also true that intimate relationships can be harmful for some people. But the reality is that the majority of people have had sexual relationships prior to marriage with no negative repercussions. For example, one study reports that when premarital sexual intercourse is satisfying, it has a positive effect on relationships for both males and females. The largest study of adult sexual behavior found that more than 90 percent of men and more than 70 percent of women recall that they wanted their first intercourse to happen when it did; only 6.9 percent of men and 21 percent of women had first intercourse on their wedding night.

The National Commission on Adolescent Sexual Health recognizes that adolescent sexuality is a highly charged emotional issue for many adults. It urges, however, that policy-makers recognize that sexual development is an essential part of adolescence and that the majority of adolescents engage in sexual behaviors as part of their overall development.

More than 50 national organizations have endorsed the Commission's consensus statement that says "society should encourage adolescents to delay sexual behaviors until they are ready physically, cognitively, and emotionally for mature sexual relationships and their consequences."

These organizations urge, however, that "society must also recognize that a majority of adolescents will become involved in sexual relationships during their teenage years. Adolescents should receive support and education for developing the skills to evaluate their readiness for mature sexual relationships."

The reality is that the majority of American adults believe that young people need to be told more than "just say no." Although 60 percent believe that premarital sexual relations for teenagers is always wrong, more than three-quarters of adults also believe that teenagers need information and access to contraceptive services and STD prevention information. Abstinence-only programs, which include misinformation about sexual behaviors and promote fear and shame, are unlikely to prove effective.

If Congress and the states are serious about helping young people delay sexual behaviors and grow into healthy, responsible adults, they will support a comprehensive approach to sexuality education that has a proven track record in accomplishing these goals.

| *"Studies have shown that sex education begun before youth are sexually active helps young people stay abstinent and use protection when they do become sexually active."*

Sex Education Programs Reduce Teen Pregnancy

Pamela DeCarlo

In the following viewpoint, Pamela DeCarlo argues that American teens have the highest rates of sexually transmitted diseases and pregnancies of any industrialized country. Therefore, she contends, the United States needs to follow the lead of other countries that have teen pregnancy rates half that of the United States and give American teenagers explicit sex and contraceptive education. Moreover, DeCarlo asserts, the earlier these programs are begun the more effective they are in convincing teens to delay sexual involvement and to protect themselves from STDs and unwanted pregnancies. DeCarlo is an AIDS researcher at the University of California in San Francisco.

As you read, consider the following questions:

1. According to DeCarlo, what percentage of teens contract HIV by the age of 22?
2. What evidence does DeCarlo present to support her contention that most young people contract HIV as teens or adolescents?
3. What are some examples of effective sex education programs, according to the author?

Fact sheet prepared by the Center for AIDS Prevention Studies (CAPS), University of California, San Francisco, June 1995. Reprinted with permission. Fact sheet available at www.caps.ucsf.edu.

Should Sex Education Be Taught in Schools?

The question is no longer *should* sex education be taught, but rather *how* should it be taught. Over 93% of all public high schools currently offer courses on sexuality or HIV. More than 510 junior or senior high schools have school-linked health clinics, and more than 300 schools make condoms available on campus. The question now is are these programs effective, and if not, how can we make them better?

Why Do Youth Need Sex Education?

Kids need the right information to help protect themselves. The United States has more than double the teenage pregnancy rate of any western industrialized country, with more than a million teenagers becoming pregnant each year. Teenagers have the highest rates of sexually transmitted diseases (STDs) of any age group, with one in four young people contracting an STD by the age of 21. STDs, including HIV, can damage teenagers' health and reproductive ability. And there is still no cure for AIDS.

HIV infection is increasing most rapidly among young people. One in four new infections in the U.S. occurs in people younger than 22. In 1994, 417 new AIDS cases were diagnosed among 13–19-year-olds, and 2,684 new cases among 20–24-year-olds. Since infection may occur up to 10 years before an AIDS diagnosis, most of those people were infected with HIV either as adolescents or pre-adolescents.

Why Has Sex Education Failed to Help Our Children?

Knowledge alone is not enough to change behaviors. Programs that rely mainly on conveying information about sex or moral precepts—how the body's sexual system functions, what teens should and shouldn't do—have failed. However, programs that focus on helping teenagers to change their behavior—using role playing, games, and exercises that strengthen social skills—have shown signs of success.

In the United States, controversy over what message should be given to children has hampered sex education programs in schools. Too often statements of values ("my children should not have sex outside of marriage") come wrapped up in misstatements of fact ("sex education doesn't work anyway"). Should we do everything possible to suppress teenage sexual behavior, or should we acknowledge that many teens are sexually active, and prepare them against the negative consequences? Emotional arguments can get in the way of an unbiased assessment of the effects of sex education.

Other countries have been much more successful than the United States in addressing the problem of teen pregnancies. Age at first intercourse is similar in the United States and five other countries: Canada, England, France, the Netherlands, and Sweden, yet all those countries have teen pregnancy rates that are at least less than half the U.S. rate. Sex education in these other countries is based on the following components: a policy explicitly favoring sex education; openness about sex; consistent messages throughout society; and access to contraception.

Often sex education curricula begin in high school, after many students have already begun experimenting sexually. Studies have shown that sex education begun before youth are sexually active helps young people stay abstinent and use protection when they do become sexually active. The sooner sex education begins, the better, even as early as elementary school.

What Kinds of Programs Work Best?

Reducing the Risk, a program for high school students in urban and rural areas in California, used behavior theory–based activities to reduce unprotected intercourse, either by helping teens avoid sex or use protection. Ninth and 10th graders attended 15 sessions as part of their regular health education classes and participated in role playing and experimental activities to build skills and self-efficacy. As a result, a greater proportion of students who were abstinent before the program successfully remained abstinent, and unprotected intercourse was significantly reduced for those students who became sexually active.

Postponing Sexual Involvement, a program for African-American 8th graders in Atlanta, Georgia, used peers (11th and 12th graders) to help youth understand social and peer pressures to have sex, and to develop and apply resistance skills. A unit of the program also taught about human sexuality, decision-making, and contraceptives. This program successfully reduced the number of abstinent students who initiated intercourse after the program, and increased contraceptive use among sexually experienced females.

Abstinence Is Not Enough

If we did a really good job in the first 10 or 12 years of children's lives teaching them about abstinence, as well as about honesty and integrity and responsibility and how to make good decisions, we would not have to be talking to them at 15 about not getting engaged in sex.

But we haven't done that. Mothers have been teaching abstinence, schools have been teaching abstinence, preachers have been preaching abstinence for years. Yet more than three million teens get STDs every year, and we still have the highest teen pregnancy, abortion, and birth rates in the industrialized world. But we seem to feel that we don't need to educate our children about their sexuality. That makes absolutely no sense. We all know the vows of abstinence break far more easily than latex condoms.

Teens need a comprehensive sexuality program that gives them all the information they need to become empowered and responsible for preventing pregnancy and disease. We have to stop trying to legislate morals and instead teach responsibility. Abstinence-only does not do that. You can't be responsible if you don't have the information.

M. Joycelyn Elders, *Rethinking Schools*, Summer 1998.

Healthy Oakland Teens (HOT) targets all 7th graders attending a junior high school in Oakland, California. Health educators teach basic sex and drug education, and 9th grade peer educators lead interactive exercises on values, decision-making, communication, and condom-use skills. After one year, students in the program were much less likely to initiate sexual activities such as deep kissing, genital touching, and sexual intercourse.

AIDS Prevention for Adolescents in School, a program for 9th and 11th graders in schools in New York City, New York, focused on correcting facts about AIDS, teaching cognitive skills to appraise risks of transmission, increasing knowledge of AIDS-prevention resources, clarifying personal values, understanding external influences, and teaching skills to delay intercourse and/or consistently use condoms. All sexually experienced students reported increased condom use after the program.

A review of 23 studies found that effective sex education programs share the following characteristics:

1. Narrow focus on reducing sexual risk-taking behaviors that may lead to HIV/STD infection or unintended pregnancy.
2. Social learning theories as a foundation for program development, focusing on recognizing social influences, changing individual values, changing group norms, and building social skills.
3. Experimental activities designed to personalize basic, accurate information about the risks of unprotected intercourse and methods of avoiding unprotected intercourse.
4. Activities that address social or media influences on sexual behaviors.
5. Reinforcing clear and appropriate values to strengthen individual values and group norms against unprotected sex.
6. Modeling and practice in communication, negotiation, and refusal skills.

What Still Needs to Be Done?

Although sex education programs in schools have been around for many years, most programs have not been nearly as effective as hoped. Schools across the country need to take a rigorous look at their programs, and begin to implement more innovative programs that have been proven effective. Educators, parents, and policy-makers should avoid emotional misconceptions about sex education; based on the rates of unwanted pregnancies and STDs including HIV among teenagers, we can no longer ignore the need for both education on how to postpone sexual involvement, and how to protect oneself when sexually active. A comprehensive risk prevention strategy uses multiple elements to protect as many of those at risk of pregnancy and STD/HIV infection as possible. Our children deserve the best education they can get.

| *"Educators knew then and know now that sex education sexualizes young children and increases sexual activity among them."*

Sex Education Programs Promote Teen Promiscuity

Joseph Collison

Joseph Collison argues in the following viewpoint that explicit sex education programs have led to a breakdown in sexual morality. The abortion and pregnancy rates of American teenagers had been declining steadily until the introduction of sex education in the schools caused them to increase sharply, he contends. Furthermore, Collison maintains, sex education supporters knew that teen abortions and teen promiscuity would increase when teens were taught sex education. Teaching sex education is a part of their plan to legitimize the sexual revolution, legalize abortion, support women's liberation, and promote the normalcy of homosexuality and other deviant sexual practices, he asserts. Collison is the director of the office of Pro-Life Activities for the diocese of Norwich, Connecticut, and chairman of the board of Caring Families Pregnancy Services.

As you read, consider the following questions:
1. How old were the students who were engaging in consensual sex in a Washington, D.C., elementary school, as cited by the author?
2. What are some of the subjects taught by the book *It's Perfectly Normal* that is used in sex education classes for 10-year-old students, according to Collison?

Reprinted with permission from "Teacher's Dirty Books," by Joseph Collison, *New Oxford Review*, January 1999. Copyright ©1999 by New Oxford Review (1069 Kains Ave., Berkeley, CA 94706).

The United States experienced a new revolution in the 1960's—FREEDOM! No more "Medieval morality!" Feel good about yourselves! Do your own thing! Children must be free to explore their world! With abortion illegitimacy would cease and there'd be no more child abuse. "Every child a wanted child," was the mantra. It would be Paradise on Earth! And the glorious freedom of youth would be guaranteed by sex education and contraceptives. "Safe sex," it was called.

A Breakdown in Morality

But the revolution has borne bitter fruit. A headline in the *Washington Post* last year reported that "Police See No Crime in School Sex Incident." Readers were informed that "D.C. police yesterday ended their investigation into a sexual incident at a Southeast Washington elementary school, concluding that a group of fourth-graders left unsupervised for up to an hour on Monday had engaged in consensual sex."

Yes, you read that right. Fourth graders were engaged in "consensual" sex, now a problem among children nationwide. The *Detroit Free Press* reported that 46 percent of fifth graders in the Detroit schools say they've engaged in sexual intercourse! In Bridgeport, Ct., 55 percent of seventh graders are sexually active.

Consider two facts: (1) Washington was the first major city in the United States to incorporate mandatory sex education into their curriculum, and (2) Washington now has the highest teen pregnancy and abortion rates in the nation. These two facts are related and they explain why, according to *USA Weekend*, one in three American children becomes sexually active before entering the eighth grade.

In the decade following Justice Harry Blackmun's discovery of strange penumbras lurking in the Constitution, sex education was instituted in schools throughout the country. Teenage pregnancies skyrocketed from 190,000 to 430,000, though the teenage population remained stable. As researchers Joseph Olsen and Stanley Weed reported in the *Wall Street Journal*, "The impact on the abortion and total pregnancy rates was exactly opposite the stated intentions of the [sex education] program."

Sex Ed Worldwide

Of course, the connection between sex-education and pregnancy, though denied by contemporary mythology, should not have been a secret. Shirley Hatley had pointed out that it was common knowledge that "In 1956, when Sweden mandated sex education, the illegitimacy rate, which had been declining, rose for every school age group except the older ones, who did not receive the special education."

Later the Swedish experience was repeated in Denmark where "illegitimate births, which were supposed to drop, instead nearly doubled; abortion rates, which were predicted to fall with the ready availability of condoms and other contraceptives in grocery stores, actually doubled; venereal disease more than doubled; and divorces doubled."

That, of course, is exactly what happened in the United States. Thomas Sowell wrote in *Forbes* magazine that "Massive, federally subsidized sex education programs entered the American public school system during the 1970's. . . . Before these programs began, teenage pregnancy was already declining for more than a decade. This long decline in teenage pregnancy then reversed and teenage pregnancies soared as 'sex education' spread pervasively throughout the public schools."

Educators knew what would happen because sex education had always been part of their agenda. As early as 1963 Alan Guttmacher, president of Planned Parenthood, wrote that contraceptive information for teens would bring about an increase in sexual promiscuity. He later explained why they wanted sex education: "The only avenue the International Planned Parenthood Federation and its allies could travel to win the battle for abortion on demand [was] through sex education."

Several years ago a minority report of the U.S. House Committee on Children, Youth, and Families pinpointed what was at the end of that avenue: "Progressively over the past 25 years we have as a nation decided that it is easier to give children pills than to teach them respect for sex and marriage. Today we are seeing the results of that decision, not only in increased pregnancy rates but in increased rates of drug abuse, venereal disease, suicide, and other forms of self-destructive behavior."

Sex Ed Increases Sexual Activity

We sowed the wind! Now we and our children have reaped the whirlwind! Not only have teenage pregnancies skyrocketed, so have abortions and divorces and venereal disease. Between 1960 and 1990:

Divorce more than doubled	up 133%
Single parent families more than tripled	up 214%
Teen suicide tripled	up 214%
Sexually transmitted diseases	up 245%
Living together without marriage	up 279%
Juvenile violent crime	up 295%
Births to unwed mothers	up 457%
Child abuse	up 500%
Abortion	up 800%

Educators knew then and know now that sex education sexualizes young children and increases sexual activity among them. A 1982 survey of 1,888 teenage women (reported in Planned Parenthood's *Family Planning Perspectives*) found that "prior exposure to a sex education course is positively and significantly associated with the initiation of sexual activity at ages 15 and 16."

Four years after that survey, William Barsiglio and Frank Mott listed "receiv[ing] education in sexual biology" among the factors causing boys to become involved in sexual intercourse at an earlier age. In the same issue Deborah Dawson emphasized that:

> It is important to note at the outset that most researchers agree that sex education does not decrease the rate of teenage pregnancies or the incidence of sexual activity. . . . The final result to emerge from the analysis is that neither pregnancy education nor contraceptive education exerts any significant effect on the risk of premarital pregnancy among sexually active teenagers, a finding that calls into question the argument that formal sex education is an effective tool for reducing adolescent pregnancy.

As a matter of fact, she did report a "significant effect." Statistical models showed that "prior contraceptive education" increases the odds of starting intercourse at age fourteen by *50 percent*.

Recently in the children's section of a large bookstore, I found *It's Perfectly Normal*, a popular elementary school sex-ed text written by Robie Harris, a member of the Planned Parenthood Board of Advocates. The book is highly recommended for ten-year-olds and contains the material recommended by the Connecticut Department of Education for fourth grade.

Over fifty graphic colored illustrations of naked boys and girls are used to discuss the normality of homosexuality and to teach little children about various sexual practices. The book shows little children how to masturbate and how to engage with others in sexual activities short of intercourse. It discusses contraceptives and illustrates how to put on condoms. It also lists nine reasons for having an abortion.

Bob Gorell. Reprinted by permission of Copley News Service.

Changing Bodies, Changing Lives is probably the most popular sex-ed text in American high schools. It teaches that "Bisexuality is an openness to loving, sexual relationships with both sexes—*our true nature*," and graphically describes sexual practices of homosexuals. Another popular text is *Learning About Sex*, touted as "A must for all young people." This textbook blithely observes that "Sado-masochism may be very acceptable and safe for sexual partners who know each other's needs."

All texts recommend fornication. *Learning About Sex* also recommends adultery: "Some people are now saying that partnerships—married or unmarried—should not be exclusive. They believe that while a primary relationship is maintained with one person, the freedom for both partners to love and share sex with others should also be present." Even bestiality is on the approved list: "A fair percentage of people probably have some sort of sexual contact with an animal during their lifetime" etc. No need here to be more explicit.

Wardell Pomeroy, author of *Boys and Sex* and *Girls and Sex* also writes of "a loving sexual relationship with an animal," but Pomeroy is more interested in simple fornication. "Premarital intercourse does have its definite values as a training ground," he says, "like taking a car out for a test run before you buy it." He neglects to mention that the majority of couples who fornicate before marriage later divorce.

After reading such books, one can understand how the schools in New Haven instituted a program to provide condoms to *fifth- and sixth-graders*. But even then, one wonders why the obvious question was never asked: "If little boys in fifth and sixth grade are given condoms, how old are the little girls the condoms will be used on?"

So what are we to do? Parents would do well to listen to the United States Centers for Disease Control, which clearly states in their publication "Condoms and Their Use in Preventing HIV Infection and Other STDs," that abstinence education is the most effective solution to unwanted pregnancy and sexual disease.

Listen to the Children

And instead of listening to the "professionals," parents should listen to their children. Few young people really want to participate in the frantic, barren games engendered by contemporary society's obsession with sex. Recently *Seventeen* magazine and the *Ms.* Foundation commissioned a nationwide study of teenage boys and girls. *Seventy-three percent* of the girls said they would have sex only if their boyfriends pressured them. The boys complained that ". . . they are pressured by their peers to have sex and are considered wimps if they don't score." *Eighty-one percent* of sexually active girls

158

said they were sorry they had become sexually active.

The last statistic agrees with a study by Dr. Marion Howard, a professor of obstetrics at Emory University in Atlanta, who surveyed a thousand teenage girls about what they most wanted to learn in their sex-education classes and found that *82 percent* said they most wanted to learn "how to say no without hurting the other person's feelings."

Of course, sex educators are zealous in safeguarding their agenda. Last year when Congress appropriated $6.7 million to teach abstinence, the White House fought hard to block the appropriation. Yet every year federal and state governments spend hundreds of millions of dollars to teach sex to our children. The Title X Adolescent Family Life program, costing *200 million dollars* a year, is but one of a number of federal programs promoting sex education and handing out contraceptives.

Deceitful Numbers

Recently the U.S. Dept. of Health and Human Services released figures documenting a drop in the teenage pregnancy rate in recent years! Immediately the Office of Population Affairs, the National Adolescent Reproductive Health Partnership, the Centers for Disease Control (publishers of the forementioned pamphlet!) and Planned Parenthood rushed to TV cameras to extol the success of sex education and the use of contraceptives, especially condoms. It was their great vindication.

But they were being deceitful. In speaking of the dramatically fewer *numbers* of teen pregnancies, they failed to mention the "Birth Dearth." In 1980 the US Census found sixteen million teenagers 14 through 17 years old; in 1990 the census found only thirteen million. There were fewer teenagers. When they also reported that the *rate* of teenage pregnancy has gone down, which is true, they failed to mention what the Consortium of State Physicians' Resource Councils detailed in "The Declines in Adolescent Pregnancy, Birth and Abortion Rates in the 1990's."

In "The Current National Picture on Teen Pregnancy," a report on the Consortium findings, Dr. Stan Weed revealed that condom use had indeed increased, but *use of the more ef-*

fective oral contraceptives had decreased to the extent that *overall contraceptive use among teens was down over 12 percent.* Furthermore, the Consortium study had separated statistics for the married teens, the sexually active unmarried teens, and the abstinent unmarried teens. Using these figures, Dr. Weed reported that the "birthrate per 1,000 sexually active [unmarried] females 15 to 19 has gone from 85.2 to 111.8 (between 1988 and 1995)—*an increase of 31.2%. And this increase occurred during the highly acclaimed increase in condom use (and commensurate but less touted decrease in pill use)."* (emphasis added)

Dr. Weed also noted that "The effort to make condoms more readily available through distribution programs has recently been tested in the Seattle Public schools. This social experiment demonstrated the fallacy of that approach. The results indicated that making condoms available to students did not increase condom use. Among students who had engaged in sex during the preceding 3 months, the percentage who used a condom actually declined from 57% to 51% among the Seattle students, and the decrease was much greater among students in schools that had clinics (and distributed more condoms) than among students in schools without clinics."

Abstinence Programs

So how can we account for the decrease in teen pregnancy? Dr. Weed explained: "For the first time in recent decades, the trend of increasing numbers of teens engaging in premarital sex has reversed. . . . The shift towards abstinent behavior [includes] awareness and concern about AIDS and other STDs. Not to be ignored in this shift, however, is the large increase in the number of teens exposed each year to programs that promote abstinence as their central message. *These programs have multiplied dramatically and account for a twelve-fold increase since 1986 in the number of teens exposed to a clear and direct message each year about sexual abstinence.* I am not aware of any other factor that might account for the shift towards abstinent behavior. (emphasis added)

There is no question that abstinence programs prevent teen pregnancy and abortion, but only if they're not diluted with contraception education. In Washington, DC, where "consensual sex" is accepted among fourth graders, 72 percent of girls are sexually active, but only one of 400 girls who participated in a "Best Friends" abstinence-only program became pregnant. The "Best Friends" abstinence program, started in Washington by Elayne Bennett, wife of former Education Secretary William Bennett, has since been successful in other cities around the country.

Father Paul Marx, the founder of Human Life International, wrote in *Faithful for Life* that "Sex desensitization turns youths into 'new age' sexual nihilists having no concept of the true nature of human sexuality. Physical sex becomes synonymous with love. Such indifferent, affectionless relations with indifferent sex partners makes sex meaningless and life empty. *Affectionate feelings and the spiritualization of sex can only be learned in a loving, cohesive family setting. Affectionate love cannot be learned from a school textbook.*"

Jennifer Grossman summed up the problem in *US News*, "People are surfeited with sex and starved for love."

| "Both safe-sex and abstinence-only activists ... have drawn—and publicized— misleading or inaccurate conclusions from the research." |

Studies Comparing Sex Education and Abstinence-Only Programs Are Inconclusive

Russell W. Gough

In the following viewpoint, Russell W. Gough asserts that both sides of the sex education debate cite studies and statistics to support the effectiveness of abstinence-only or comprehensive sex education programs. However, Gough contends, the research available on the different sex education programs is too tentative and preliminary to offer any firm conclusions on the effectiveness of any particular program. Gough is a professor of philosophy and ethics at Pepperdine University and the author of *Character Is Destiny: The Value of Personal Ethics in Everyday Life.*

As you read, consider the following questions:
1. What two points are to be emphasized by the new federally mandated abstinence-only sex education programs, according to the author?
2. What evidence does Gough present to support his claim that both sides of the sex education debate publish misleading or inaccurate claims to support their views?

From "Does Abstinence Education Work?" by Russell W. Gough. This article originally appeared in the August 1997 issue and is reprinted with permission from *The World & I*, a publication of The Washington Times Corporation, copyright ©1997.

C lashes over school-based sex-education programs have erupted like volcanoes over the past decade. Each side has cited statistics and made claims to back up its position, and has jockeyed for attention in newspaper articles, op-ed columns, and TV broadcasts.

Abstinence Versus Comprehensive Sex Education

But which side's program *really works:* sexual-abstinence education, or "comprehensive" sex ed, which teaches the abstinence option as part of a broadbrush treatment of sexual issues, including contraception, abortion, and homosexuality?

The public-health and family problems confronting society today are stark and disturbing: Over 1 million teenage girls a year become pregnant (with 65 percent of the resulting babies born out of wedlock).

Moreover, 3 million teens acquire a sexually transmitted disease each year (which translates into 1 out of every 10 adolescents).

While virtually all Americans agree that some form of proactive and preventive educational measures are necessary to address these invidious problems, varied and passionate opinions exist as to precisely what form sex-education curricula should take.

The reason is that this debate often entails deeply diverging and divisive value-based viewpoints on human development, sexual identity, lifestyle, and abortion.

Indeed, the battle cry rhetoric over how to best address the alarming rates of teen pregnancy and sexually transmitted diseases (STDs) crescendoed to an all-time high in March 1997. At that time, the federal government announced it would spend $250 million over five years to promote abstinence-only education programs.

The federally mandated initiative is designed to teach young Americans that:
• sex before marriage "is likely to have harmful psychological and physical effects" and
• avoidance of extramarital sex "is the expected standard" of human behavior.

The legislation, initiated by Congress and signed into law by President Clinton, represents the largest effort ever undertaken by the federal government to promote sexual abstinence outside marriage.

A total of $50 million a year will be automatically released beginning October 1 [1997] to states that apply for it and provide a 75 percent match. (That is, states must provide $3 for every $4 from the federal government.) The program is widely expected to spawn numerous abstinence-only courses nationwide.

Culture Clash

Critics of the abstinence-only measure quickly sought to drive home one overarching rejoinder: Sufficient scientific evidence does not exist to demonstrate that abstinence-only programs work. Thus, it was argued, allocating such a large sum of money to such dubious educational programs is scientifically unfounded at best and irresponsibly wasteful at worst.

It would be far wiser and empirically sound, the critics said, to invest in "comprehensive" sex education programs that emphasize "safe sex" or "safer sex" instruction—practical information on birth control (condom use in particular), various sexual options, and the like—and at the same time teach the advantages of abstinence.

Besides, the critics added, in a significant number of cases it is highly unrealistic to expect teenagers to practice abstinence. Many teens will engage in sex no matter how much we encourage them to abstain, so we are better off providing them with the know-how to have sex safely.

On the other side of the issue, supporters of the federal initiative defended its political merit and educational necessity primarily on the basis of one largely unarguable piece of evidence: The conventional "safe sex" education programs of the past two decades have not lowered the rates of teen pregnancy and STDs.

Such programs have failed in large measure, it was argued further, because of their self-defeating premise that "teens are going to do it anyway." As a result, these programs primarily and often exclusively made it their goal to teach teens how to have sex safely (to prevent STDs) and responsibly (to avoid pregnancy) instead of establishing abstinence as a central aim.

In notable fact, no school-based abstinence-oriented curricula existed prior to the late 1980s. Conventional "safe sex" programs did not emphasize abstinence until after the discovery of the AIDS virus.

Given that the rates of teen pregnancy and STDs have clearly not been reduced, supporters of the legislation said, it is high time to try a different model of sex education—the abstinence-only approach. Besides, to tell teens, "Don't have sex, but here's how to do it safely," sends a mixed message and is tantamount to encouraging sexual activity.

Accordingly, those who espouse the first general rhetorical argument are advocates of what is usually described as the "safe-sex," "safer-sex," or "comprehensive" approach to sex education. And those who espouse the second general rhetorical argument are advocates of what is variously described as the "abstinence-only," "abstinence," "abstinence-based," or "abstinence-oriented" approach to sex education.

Notably, the latter two labels typically suggest that, while some information regarding contraception use is or may be appropriate for certain age levels, abstinence should be the central and guiding ideal of any sex-ed program. (These latter two labels, however, are now often used by "safe sex" or "comprehensive" programs to convey that abstinence instruction is a part of their curricula.)

Scant Scientific Research

These two arguments on either side of the federal government's $250 million abstinence-only campaign inevitably press us—policymakers, educators, parents, and concerned citizens alike—to ask the following bedrock question: Rhetoric aside, which approach is most supported by the scientific research regarding sex education?

To be sure, this is a critical question that deserves—indeed, requires—a conscientious and decisive response. At present, however, only a conscientious response is available: The reliable scientific research to date is far too scant and preliminary to offer us any overarchingly confident, much less decisive, answers concerning the effectiveness of school-based sex-education programs.

Beyond the few and strikingly insufficient studies that exist, there is only quasiscientific or anecdotal evidence—which, to be sure, is plentiful on both sides of the debate and which does count for something but is not the focus here. The focus is on the "reliable scientific research," by which is meant methodologically rigorous studies. According to Douglas Kirby, a leading researcher in this field, a sound study should:

- evaluate a sufficient number of representative programs;
- use random assignment;
- include a sufficiently large sample size;
- conduct long-term follow-up;
- measure behavior rather than just attitudes or beliefs;
- conduct proper statistical analyses;
- publish both positive and negative results;
- replicate studies of successful programs; and
- use independent evaluators.

In 1994, in the most comprehensive review to date of the relevant research, Kirby and eight colleagues attempted to assess the effectiveness of 23 studies of school-based sex-education programs that had been published in professional, peer-reviewed journals.

Among the studies, the researchers identified 7 that were based on national surveys and 16 that evaluated the impact of specific programs. Of the latter, the researchers identified 13 studies of "safe sex" or "comprehensive" sex-education programs, and, notably, a mere 3 studies involving school-based abstinence-only programs (which should not be surprising, given that such programs have only been in existence since the late 1980s).

Tentative Conclusions Emerge

In summarizing their assessment of the 23 studies, Kirby and his colleagues importantly concluded, "There are serious limitations in the research on pregnancy prevention programs, and little is known with much certainty." They nonetheless went on to offer the following noteworthy—but largely tentative—observations about the impact of such programs:

- The studies that were reviewed show that programs involving both abstinence and STD, HIV/AIDS, and contraception education "do not increase sexual activity."

• The seven national surveys suggest that sex-education programs "do increase the use of contraceptives and AIDS education programs do increase the use of condoms somewhat. However, the data are not always consistent."

• "To date, the published literature does not provide any good evidence indicating whether programs focusing only upon abstinence either do or do not delay the onset of intercourse or reduce the frequency of intercourse."

• The few programs that delayed the onset of intercourse, increased the use of condoms or other contraceptives, or reduced risky sexual behaviors had six common characteristics:

1. "theoretical grounding in social-learning or social-influence theories";
2. "a narrow focus on reducing specific sexual risk-taking behaviors";
3. "experiential activities to convey the information on the risks of unprotected sex and how to avoid those risks and to personalize that information";
4. "instruction on social influences and pressures";
5. "reinforcement of individual values and group norms against unprotected sex that are age and experience appropriate"; and
6. "activities to increase relevant skills and confidence in those skills."

Making Sense of the Research

As with most social scientific studies and data, however, a few important words of caution are in order here, for these types of "facts" do not speak for themselves but require a great deal of interpretation, context, and qualification.

First and foremost, as Kirby and his colleagues make quite clear, their "conclusions" at present are tentative and preliminary at best.

"Our ability to reach definitive conclusions," they said, "was limited by the few rigorous studies of individual programs, by methodological limitations of individual studies, and by inconsistent results among some of the findings. Additional research needs to employ more valid and statistically powerful methods."

As such, one could understandably and fairly infer that the

167

existing scientific literature examining the effectiveness of school-based sex-education programs cannot and should not be used as a rhetorical or political trump card, to say the least.

Second, both safe-sex and abstinence-only activists (to the chagrin of researchers) have drawn—and publicized—misleading or inaccurate conclusions from the research Kirby and his colleagues conducted.

For example, a number of abstinence-only advocates have inferred that safe-sex programs promote increased sexual activity among teens, given that the research indicates such programs increase the use of contraceptives. This does not necessarily follow, of course, as Kirby and his colleagues point out: It may be the case that safe-sex programs do not increase sexual activity and at the same time do increase the use of condoms (among those who are already sexually active, that is).

On the other side, those opposed to abstinence-only curricula continue to argue, citing the Kirby study as "proof," that abstinence-only programs "do not work." But the Kirby study clearly does not demonstrate this assertion.

Reading, 'Riting, and Sex Ed

• "Comprehensive" sex-education curricula emphasize "safe sex" instruction that includes practical information on birth control (condom use in particular) and various sexual options.

• These programs have failed to lower the rates of teen pregnancy and STDs over the past two decades.

• Abstinence-only sex-ed programs strive primarily or exclusively to teach young people how to postpone sexual activity until marriage.

• Reliable scientific studies are still too few and preliminary to tell which approach works best.

Russell W. Gough, *World & I*, August 1997, p. 60.

The most significant conclusion Kirby and his associates drew concerning the effectiveness of abstinence-only programs is that, given the paucity and incompleteness of existing scholarly research on such programs (which, in turn, is largely due to the very recent advent of such programs), one cannot presently say with any empirical confidence to what extent they are or are not effective. Scientifically speaking, we simply don't know yet.

Third, and significantly, an inescapable philosophical point that undergirds the scientific issue is this: It makes no small difference how researchers (much less policymakers and political activists) define the concept of "effectiveness."

For example, in their comprehensive study, Kirby and his associates—consistent with "safe sex" or "comprehensive" sex-ed advocates but not with most "abstinence-only" or "abstinence-primarily" advocates—define "effectiveness" quite narrowly (and, I should be quick to add, understandably for empirical purposes) in terms of reducing teen pregnancies and STDs. But many individuals and groups that back abstinence instruction tend to construe "effectiveness" in terms of a broader range of outcomes—not merely the physical-health outcomes of reducing teen pregnancies and STDs but also outcomes related to emotional, psychological, spiritual, and "character" consequences.

Thus, even if future, Kirby-like studies produce new evidence that abstinence-only programs "do not work," there would nonetheless remain the complex and consequential issue of how best to define "effectiveness."

About Values More than Science

This philosophical point leads to a fourth and final observation concerning the past, present, and even future scientific research on school-based sex-education programs.

The question of how best to define "effectiveness" is at bottom a question of value-laden guiding philosophies. And as such, it is a question that cannot exclusively or even primarily be settled by empirical investigation—although it certainly can and should be informed by such investigation.

The final arbiter will thus have to be the prevailing moral and philosophical convictions of the American public. Indeed, the issue of sex education so thoroughly and necessarily entails value-laden assumptions concerning human development, sexual identity and lifestyle, personal character, and rights and responsibilities that it is highly doubtful that researchers can conduct their investigations into the "effectiveness" of school-based sex-education programs free of such assumptions.

If they can't, this would by no means render their research worthless. It would suggest, however, that in many cases researchers—several of whom, including Kirby, publicly decried the recent federally mandated abstinence-only initiative for lacking sufficient empirical support—themselves may not be evaluating, and perhaps cannot evaluate, these programs in the roles of completely neutral, disinterested observers.

Quantifying the statistical regularities of teen pregnancy and STDs is one thing. But evaluating how best to educate teens about their sexual identity, development, and behavior is quite another—a necessarily and deeply value-laden thing.

Periodical Bibliography

The following articles have been selected to supplement the diverse views presented in this chapter. Addresses are provided for periodicals not indexed in the *Readers' Guide to Periodical Literature*, the *Alternative Press Index*, the *Social Sciences Index*, or the *Index to Legal Periodicals and Books*.

Richard Cohen	"The Abstinence Candidate," *Washington Post*, June 24, 1999.
Adam Davidson	"The Joy of No Sex," *Rolling Stone*, October 15, 1998.
Candace de Russy	"Sex and Bondage 101," *Women's Quarterly*, Summer 1998.
Education Digest	"Curricular Programs to Curb Teen Pregnancy," March 1999.
M. Joycelyn Elders	"Respect Your Elders!" *Poz*, December 1997. Available from 349 W. 12th St., New York, NY 10014-1721.
Amitai Etzioni	"Education for Intimacy," *Tikkun*, March/April 1997.
Marilyn Gardner	"Shifts in Sex Ed—Talking Abstinence," *Christian Science Monitor*, August 11, 1998.
Debra W. Haffner	"Sexuality Education," *Social Policy*, Spring 1998.
Robert H. Knight	"A Gay Video for Schoolkids," *Weekly Standard*, April 7, 1997. Available from PO Box 710, Radnor, PA 19088-0710.
Jodie Morse	"Preaching Chastity in the Classroom," *Time*, October 18, 1999.
Priscilla Pardini	"Federal Law Mandates 'Abstinence-Only' Sex Ed," *Rethinking Schools*, Summer 1998.
Annys Shin	"Empower Program May Prove Too Hot to Handle," *Ms.*, July/August 1998.
Gary Thomas	"Where True Love Waits," *Christianity Today*, March 1, 1999.

For Further Discussion

Chapter 1

1. Tamar Lewin reports that many teens consider oral sex a safer and less intimate alternative to intercourse. Do you agree with the teens she interviewed? Why or why not?

2. Joshua Harris argues that dating should be discouraged because its purpose is to encourage intimacy, which he believes should be reserved for marriage. Do you agree with his argument? Why or why not? In your opinion, what is the purpose of dating? If a couple is dating, does that mean they are or should be sexually intimate?

3. This chapter presents a wide range of opinions on what influences teen sexual behavior. Consider each argument, then rank each factor in order of strongest to weakest influence on teen sexual behavior. Explain your rankings. If you do not believe a viewpoint should not be included in the ranking, explain why. If there are other influences that you believe should be listed, include them and explain why.

Chapter 2

1. Rebecca A. Maynard and Kristin Luker debate the seriousness and consequences of teen pregnancy on teens, their children, and society. Compare and contrast their visions for the future of pregnant teens and their children.

2. Oliver Starr Jr. is a freelance writer who contends that older men are responsible for a large percentage of teen births, while Kristin A. Moore and Anne Driscoll, experts in the field of teen pregnancy, maintain that teen girls and their first sexual partners are close in age. On what points do they agree? Which of their arguments is more convincing, and why? Does knowing their backgrounds influence your assessment of their arguments? Explain your answer.

Chapter 3

1. William F. Buckley contends that minor teens will stop having sex if they know they will be prosecuted for fornication or statutory rape. Robin Abcarian argues, on the other hand, that such prosecutions will not reduce the teen sex rate but will cause teen girls to hide their pregnancies or abandon their newborn babies. In your opinion, do you think prosecuting minor teens for fornication or statutory rape is an effective means of lowering the teen sex rate? Why or why not?

2. Bruce A. Lucero, Bill Bell, and Karen Bell argue the pros and cons of parental notification laws for teen abortions. If states require parental consent in order to give a teen an aspirin at school, should parental notification or consent be required for a teen to have an abortion? Why or why not? Some states also require doctors and clinics to have parental consent before they give contraceptives or reproductive health services to minor teens. Do you agree with this policy? Why or why not? How much control should parents have over their minor daughter's decisions? What if the daughter's decision conflicts with that of her parents'? Explain your answers.

3. Maggie Gallagher declares that teen pregnancy would be less of a problem if the teen parents were married. Melissa Ludtke counters that teen marriages are not always beneficial for either the teens or their offspring. Based on your readings in this book, do you think pregnant teen girls should be encouraged to marry their babies' fathers? Why or why not?

Chapter 4

1. Joe S. McIlhaney Jr. argues that when teens are given all the information about the dangers and risks of sexual activity and the failure rates of contraceptives, they will understand that abstinence is the healthiest option for them. How does Debra W. Haffner respond to this argument? Based on your reading of the viewpoints in this chapter, what type of sex education should be taught in schools? Explain your answer.

2. Joseph Collison blames the introduction of explicit sex education into the classroom for the loss of sexual morals, the rising teen pregnancy and abortion rates, and for society's acceptance of homosexuality. What evidence does Collison present to support his views? Is his argument convincing? Why or why not?

3. According to Russell W. Gough, activists for both abstinence-only and comprehensive sex education programs draw misleading and inaccurate conclusions from research conducted by Douglas Kirby to support their claims about the efficacy of different sex education programs. Using Gough's viewpoint as a guide, find examples in the chapter viewpoints where the facts have been misrepresented.

Organizations to Contact

The editors have compiled the following list of organizations concerned with the issues debated in this book. The descriptions are derived from materials provided by the organizations. All have publications or information available for interested readers. The list was compiled on the date of publication of the present volume; the information provided here may change. Be aware that many organizations take several weeks or longer to respond to inquiries, so allow as much time as possible.

Advocates for Youth
1025 Vermont Ave. NW, Ste. 200, Washington, DC 20005
(202) 347-5700 • fax: (202) 347-2263
e-mail: info@advocatesforyouth.org
website: www.advocatesforyouth.org

Advocates for Youth is the only national organization focusing solely on pregnancy and HIV prevention among young people. It provides information, education, and advocacy to youth-serving agencies and professionals, policy makers, and the media. Among the organization's numerous publications are the brochures *Advice from Teens on Buying Condoms* and *Spread the Word—Not the Virus* and the pamphlet *How to Prevent Date Rape: Teen Tips.*

Alan Guttmacher Institute
120 Wall St., Washington, DC 10005
(212) 248-1111 • fax: (212) 248-1951
e-mail: info@agi-usa.org • website: www.agi-usa.org

The institute works to protect and expand the reproductive choices of all women and men. It strives to ensure that people have access to the information and services they need to exercise their rights and responsibilities concerning sexual activity, reproduction, and family planning. Among the institute's publications are the books *Teenage Pregnancy in Industrialized Countries* and *Today's Adolescents, Tomorrow's Parents: A Portrait of the Americas* and the report "Sex and America's Teenagers."

American Civil Liberties Union (ACLU)
125 Broad St., 18th Fl., New York, NY 10004
(212) 549-2500 • fax: (212) 549-2646
website: www.aclu.org

The ACLU is a national organization that works to defend Americans' civil rights as guaranteed by the U.S. Constitution. It supports confidential reproductive health care for teens and civil rights for homosexuals. ACLU publications include the monthly *Civil Liberties Alert*, the quarterly newsletter *Civil Liberties*, the briefing paper "Reproductive Freedom: The Rights of Minors," as well as handbooks and pamphlets.

Child Trends, Inc. (CT)
4301 Connecticut Ave. NW, Ste. 100, Washington, DC 20008
(202) 362-5580 • fax: (202) 362-5533
e-mail: swilliams@childtrends.org
website: www.childtrends.org

CT works to provide accurate statistical and research information regarding children and their families in the United States and to educate the American public on the ways existing social trends, such as the increasing rate of teenage pregnancy, affect children. In addition to the annual newsletter *Facts at a Glance*, which presents the latest data on teen pregnancy rates for every state, CT also publishes the papers "Next-Steps and Best Bets: Approaches to Preventing Adolescent Childbearing" and "Welfare and Adolescent Sex: The Effects of Family History, Benefit Levels, and Community Context."

Coalition for Positive Sexuality (CPS)
3712 N. Broadway, PMB #191, Chicago, IL 60613
(773) 604-1654
website: www.positive.org

The Coalition for Positive Sexuality is a grassroots direct-action group formed in the spring of 1992 by high school students and activists. CPS works to counteract the institutionalized misogyny, heterosexism, homophobia, racism, and ageism that students experience every day at school. It is dedicated to offering teens sexuality and safe sex education that is pro-woman, pro-lesbian/gay/bisexual, pro-safe sex, and pro-choice. Its motto is, "Have fun and be safe." CPS publishes the pamphlet *Just Say Yes*.

Family Research Council (FRC)
801 G St. NW, Washington, DC 20001
(202) 393-2100 • fax: (202) 393-2134
e-mail: corrdept@frc.org • website: www.frc.org

The council is a research, resource, and education organization that promotes the traditional family, which the council defines as a group of people bound by marriage, blood, or adoption. It opposes schools' tolerance of homosexuality and condom distribution programs in schools. It also believes that pornography breaks up marriages and contributes to sexual violence. Among the council's numerous publications are the papers "Revolt of the Virgins," "Abstinence: The New Sexual Revolution," and "Abstinence Programs Show Promise in Reducing Sexual Activity and Pregnancy Among Teens."

Family Resource Coalition of America (FRCA)
20 N. Wacker Dr., Ste. 1100, Chicago, IL 60606
(312) 338-0900 • fax: (312) 338-1522
website: www.frca.org

FRCA is a national consulting and advocacy organization that seeks to strengthen and empower families and communities so they can foster the optimal development of children, teenagers, and adult family members. FRCA publishes the bimonthly newsletter *Connection*, the report "Family Involvement in Adolescent Pregnancy and Parenting Programs," and the fact sheet "Family Support Programs and Teen Parents."

Focus on the Family
Colorado Springs, CO 80995
(719) 531-5181 • fax: (719) 531-3424
website: www.fotf.org

Focus on the Family is an organization that promotes Christian values and strong family ties and that campaigns against pornography and homosexual rights laws. It publishes the monthly magazine *Focus on the Family* and the books *Love Won Out: A Remarkable Journey Out of Homosexuality* and *No Apologies . . . the Truth About Life, Love, and Sex.*

The Heritage Foundation
214 Massachusetts Ave. NE, Washington, DC 20002-4999
(202) 546-4400 • fax: (202) 546-8328
e-mail: info@heritage.org • website: www.heritage.org

The Heritage Foundation is a public policy research institute that supports the ideas of limited government and the free-market system. It promotes the view that the welfare system has contributed to the problems of illegitimacy and teenage pregnancy. Among the foundation's numerous publications is its Backgrounder series, which includes "Liberal Welfare Programs: What the Data Show on Programs for Teenage Mothers," the paper "Rising Illegitimacy: America's Social Catastrophe," and the bulletin "How Congress Can Protect the Rights of Parents to Raise Their Children."

National Campaign to Prevent Teen Pregnancy
21 M St. NW, Ste. 300, Washington, DC 20037
(202) 261-5655
website: www.teenpregnancy.org

The mission of the National Campaign is to reduce teenage pregnancy by promoting values and activities that are consistent with a pregnancy-free adolescence. The campaign's goal is to reduce the pregnancy rate among teenage girls by one-third by the year 2005. The campaign publishes pamphlets, brochures, and opinion polls that include *No Easy Answers: Research Finding on Programs to Reduce Teen Pregnancy, Not Just for Girls: Involving Boys and Men in Teen Pregnancy Prevention,* and *Public Opinion Polls and Teen Pregnancy.*

National Organization on Adolescent Pregnancy, Parenting, and Prevention (NOAPPP)
2401 Pennsylvania Ave., Ste. 350, Washington, DC 20037
(202) 293-8370
e-mail: noappp@noappp.org • website: www.noappp.org

NOAPPP promotes comprehensive and coordinated services designed for the prevention and resolution of problems associated with adolescent pregnancy and parenthood. It supports families in setting standards that encourage the healthy development of children through loving, stable, relationships. NOAPPP publishes the quarterly *NOAPPP Network Newsletter* and various fact sheets on teen pregnancy.

Planned Parenthood Federation of America (PPFA)
810 7th Ave., New York, NY 10019
(212) 541-7800 • (212) 245-1845
e-mail: communications@ppfa.org
website: www.plannedparenthood.org

Planned Parenthood believes individuals have the right to control their own fertility without governmental interference. It promotes comprehensive sex education and provides contraceptive counseling and services through clinics across the United States. Its publications include the brochures *Guide to Birth Control: Seven Accepted Methods of Contraception, Teen Sex? It's Okay to Say No Way,* and the bimonthly newsletter *LinkLine.*

Project Reality
PO Box 97, Golf, IL 60029-0097
(847)729-3298
e-mail: preality@pair.com
website: www.project-reality.pair.com

Project Reality has developed a sex education curriculum for junior and senior high students called Sex Respect. The program is designed to provide teenagers with information and to encourage sexual abstinence.

Sex Information and Education Council of Canada (SIECCAN)
850 Coxwell Ave., Toronto, ON M4C 5R1 Canada
(416) 466-5304 • fax: (416) 778-0785
e-mail: sieccan@web.net • website: www.sieccan.org

SIECCAN conducts research on sexual health and sexuality education. It publishes the *Canadian Journal of Human Sexuality* and the resource document *Common Questions About Sexual Health Education*, and maintains an information service for health professionals.

Sexuality Information and Education Council of the United States (SIECUS)
130 W. 42nd St., Ste. 350, New York, NY 10036-7802
(212) 819-9770 • fax: (212) 819-9776
e-mail: siecus@siecus.org • website: www.siecus.org

SIECUS is an organization of educators, physicians, social workers, and others who support the individual's right to acquire knowledge of sexuality and who encourage responsible sexual behavior. The council promotes comprehensive sex education for all children that includes AIDS education, teaching about homosexuality, and instruction about contraceptives and sexually transmitted diseases. Its publications include fact sheets, annotated bibliographies by topic, the booklet *Talk About Sex*, and the monthly *SIECUS Report*.

Teen-Aid
723 E. Jackson Ave., Spokane, WA 99207
(509) 482-2868 • fax: (509) 482-7994
e-mail: teenaid@teen-aid.org • website: www.teen-aid.org

Teen-Aid is an international organization that promotes traditional family values and sexual morality. It publishes a public school sex education curriculum, *Sexuality, Commitment and Family*, stressing sexual abstinence before marriage.

Bibliography of Books

Susie Bright   *Susie Bright's Sexual State of the Union*. New York: Simon & Schuster, 1997.

Robert Coles   *The Youngest Parents: Teenage Pregnancy as It Shapes Lives*. New York: Norton, 1997.

Paula Edelson   *Straight Talk About Teenage Pregnancy*. New York: Facts On File, 1999.

Julie Endersbe   *Homosexuality: What Does It Mean?* Mankato, MN: LifeMatters, 2000.

Julie Endersbe   *Teen Sex: Risks and Consequences*. Mankato, MN: LifeMatters, 2000.

Joshua Harris   *I Kissed Dating Goodbye*. Sisters, OR: Multnomah Publishers, 1997.

Kate Havelin   *Dating: What Is a Healthy Relationship?* Mankato, MN: LifeMatters, 2000.

Thomas Hine   *The Rise and Fall of the American Teenager*. New York: Bard, 1999.

Ruth Horowitz   *Teen Mothers—Citizens or Dependents?* Chicago: University of Chicago Press, 1995.

Elaine Bell Kaplan   *Not Our Kind of Girl: Unraveling the Myths of Black Teenage Motherhood*. Berkeley: University of California Press, 1997.

Anna Kreiner   *In Control: Learning to Say No to Sexual Pressure*. New York. Rosen Publishing Group, 1997.

Melissa Ludtke   *On Our Own: Unmarried Motherhood in America*. New York: Random House, 1997.

Kristin Luker   *Dubious Conceptions: The Politics of Teenage Pregnancy*. Cambridge, MA: Harvard University Press, 1996.

Rebecca A. Maynard, ed.   *Kids Having Kids: Economic Costs and Social Consequences of Teen Pregnancy*. New York: Robin Hood Foundation, 1996.

Richard A. Panzer   *Condom Nation: Blind Faith, Bad Science*. Westwood, NJ: Center for Educational Media, 1997.

Lynn E. Ponton   *The Romance of Risk: Why Teenagers Do the Things They Do*. New York: BasicBooks, 1997.

Judith E. Reisman   *Kinsey: Crimes and Consequences*. Arlington, VA: Institute for Media Education, 1998.

Katie Roiphe   *Last Night in Paradise: Sex and Morals at the Century's End*. Boston: Little, Brown, 1997.

Wendy Shalit   *A Return to Modesty: Discovering Lost Virtue.*
                      New York: Free Press, 1999.

Leora Tanenbaum   *Slut! Growing Up Female with a Bad Reputation.*
                      New York: Seven Stories Press, 1999.

Naomi Wolf   *Promiscuities: The Secret Struggle for Womanhood.*
                      New York: Random House, 1997.

Index

184